A RING OF WESSE

An Angler's R

Palladian Bridge at Wilton   *Painting by Paul Stewart*

JOHN ASHLEY-COOPER

A Ring
of
Wessex Waters

An Angler's Rivers

ILLUSTRATED WITH 13 COLOUR PLATES
AND 72 TEXT PHOTOGRAPHS

H. F. & G. WITHERBY LTD.

First published in Great Britain 1986
First paperback edition published 1990 by
H. F. & G. WITHERBY LTD
14 Henrietta Street, London WC2E 8QJ

British Library Cataloguing in Publication Data
Ashley-Cooper, John
    A ring of Wessex waters.
    1. South-West England. Angling
    I. Title
    799.1209423

    ISBN 0-85493-198-8

Filmset in Monophoto 13pt Apollo
and printed in Great Britain by
BAS Printers Limited,
Over Wallop, Hampshire

Foreword
BY THE HON. AYLMER TRYON

John Ashley-Cooper's home was on the family estate at Wimborne St. Giles on a high point with a magnificent view to the south as far as Badbury Rings and on a clear day to the Purbeck Hills beyond. He delighted to point out where lay the rivers described in this book. Each of these has a character of its own, and in many respects the fish, flora and bird life, and perhaps humans too, vary with their individual valleys.

The author was probably the greatest salmon fisherman of his generation, and certainly the most knowledgeable. He devoted much of his life after the war to the Art of fishing, and to the study of fish in their respective rivers; especially the salmon. It was said that whilst a prisoner of war he had decided that this would be his vocation, and this book is the culmination of that resolve; having previously given us his thoughts in *The Great Salmon Rivers of Scotland* and later in *A Salmon Fisher's Odyssey* and *A Line on Salmon*.

This scholarly book transports us as in a dream boat, from source to estuary, telling us as we glide along, not only of the fish and their fluctuating fortunes, but also of the history of the ancient towns through which we pass, and the life of the surrounding water meadows.

John Ashley-Cooper was the most unselfish and considerate of fishing companions, and his descriptions of the best methods for each river reflect his modesty and love of the subject. Those of us who were privileged to fish with him, when sport was poor and rivers too low or too high, were encouraged by his enthusiasm and tales of better times.

His initiation into the arts of salmon fishing came from the great fisherman Hardy Corfe. Perhaps it is no coincidence that another great fisherman, the Canadian author Roderick Haig-Brown, should have learnt from a stern tutor also on the Frome where he caught his first salmon, as described in *A River Never Sleeps*.

We are thankful that the author had completed *A Ring of Wessex Waters* before his death after his 'last cast' and a happy day's fishing on the river Bolstad in Norway, the haunt of leviathans. Certainly a contrast in scenery to our Wessex waters, but then the author enjoyed all salmon rivers in the company of his many fishing friends and his books will always recall those days and bring happy memories to us and a fund of knowledge, so modestly told to future generations as well.

Author's Preface

'Are not Abana and Pharpar, rivers of Damascus, better than all the waters of Israel?' (2 Kings v. 12). So protested the Syrian general Naaman to the prophet Elisha, 'as every schoolboy knows', (or at least every divinity student). This is without doubt the earliest known comparison of one river or set of rivers with another. Comparisons proverbially are odious, a truism applicable to chalk streams as to many other subjects; yet why has so much been written (and justly so) about those famous waters of Itchen and Test, and so little by comparison about their sister rivers, Avon, Frome, and Piddle, let alone Nadder, Wylye, Ebble, and others? It is in an effort towards rectifying this omission that this present book largely owes its origin.

It has rightly been written: 'Every river has its own quality, and it is part of wisdom to know and love as many as you can'. It is certainly also true, as has often been pointed out, that there is more to fishing than the catching of fish. In addition, although fishing of one sort or another may well be the main riverside activity in this present era, there is also much more to the story of rivers than the mere account of their fishings and their fish. Rivers are the waterways of history in more than one sense. They existed long before the evolution of mankind upon this planet, and will doubtless still be flowing long after his disappearance from it.

For these reasons the author has endeavoured in this book to cast a net over wider topics than fishing and fish, however absorbing their study may be. He has attempted a description of the course and surroundings of various south country rivers in Wiltshire, Hampshire, and Dorset; also of some of the towns and villages past or through which they flow.

Some account of historical events that have taken place on their banks has also been included, as well as of other features of interest such as the wildlife of their neighbourhood.

As a result of this the reader may well be inclined to wonder whether he has taken up a fishing book, a guide book, or a history book; and he may justly consider it a combination of all three.

Even for those whose interest lies mainly in fishing, the most dedicated angler, not least the dry-fly fisherman who inevitably spends much leisure time waiting for a hatch of fly, may perhaps find enough in such diverse matters to interest him?

It is much hoped in addition that this book may engage the attention, not only of the angler, but of anyone who holds in affection the enchanting Wessex countryside and its story. If it seems peculiar, therefore, to find a book embracing such dissimilar topics as, say, the localities of salmon or trout spawning beds at one moment coupled with the history of Roman remains at another, the above is the train of thought which has given rise to such diversity. The author trusts his readers will accept this with sympathy, or at least in a spirit of tolerance.

On the Little Durnford water

Contents

Good Dorset names

Colour Plates

Acknowledgements

The Author wished to record his grateful appreciation to the following for the advice, assistance and information which they kindly provided during the book's preparation:—

Mr. L. U. Borenius, Mr. T. J. Caines, Mr. J. Chichester, Mr. A. J. Cherry, Lt. Cdr. H. M. Darlow R.N., Brigadier S. N. Floyer Acland, Capt. P. Green, Sir Michael Hanham, Viscount Head, Mr. P. Lapsley, Cdr. G. Marten R.N. and the Hon. Mrs Marten, Lady Mills, Major J. Mills, Mr J. C. S. Mills, Mr. D. A. Nickol, The Earl of Normanton, Mr. M. Parker, The Earl of Pembroke and Montgomery, Major General M. D. Price, Mrs. Radclyffe, Major D. A. C. Rasch, Mr. T. Rickard (Wiltshire Fisheries Association), Mr. C. Rothwell (Frome and Piddle Association), Major D. H. Scarfe (Services Dry Fly Fishing Association), The Earl of Shaftesbury, The Hon. A. Tryon, The Lord Tryon, Dr. D. R. Wilkinson (Wessex Water Authority) and Mr. H. Wood-Homer.

Thanks were also due to the late Mr. P. Brown, the late Mr. A. E. Wallace Tarry, and the late Colonel J. Walker for their help.

The paintings in the book are the work of Mr. Paul Stewart.

The photograph of Capt. Radclyffe's retriever on page 207 is reproduced from Sir Herbert Maxwell's *Fishing at Home and Abroad* (1913).

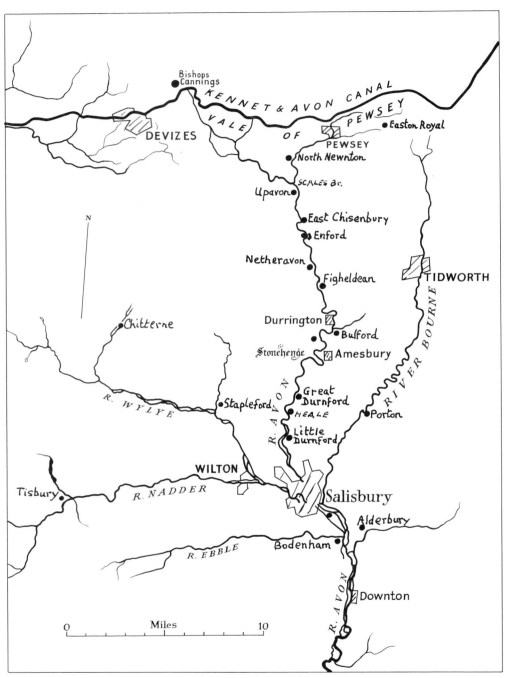

UPPER AVON

THE AVON

From Source To Salisbury (Upper Avon)

The name 'Avon' is said to be derived from a Celtic word meaning 'water'. This is quite likely the case, as there are no less than nine rivers of this name, spread over various parts of Britain. Three Avons are in Scotland, one a tributary of the Spey, one of the Clyde, and one of the Forth. In Wales there are two, which flow into Swansea Bay. In England there is the Warwickshire Avon, the Bristol Avon, the Devonshire Avon, and above all the Wiltshire or Hampshire Avon, featuring prominently in this book. The name is therefore a much used one, dating in all probability from pre-historic times.

It is customary, when describing rivers, to start at their source and work downstream. This is perhaps the easiest as well as the traditional method, so it will be followed here.

This great river, the Wiltshire Avon, rises in the vale of Pewsey on the south side of the Marlborough downs. There are in fact two headwaters, the East Avon and the West Avon, while a third brook joins the East Avon close to North Newnton. It is splitting hairs to argue which of these headwaters is the main Avon, and they converge at Scales Bridge about half a mile above the village of Upavon, four miles south of Pewsey. Both East and West branches are similar in size, in fact little bigger than modest sized brooks. The East branch rises near Easton Royal about three miles east of Pewsey, and the West branch near Bishop's Cannings about three miles north east of Devizes.

There is little out of the ordinary about these sources, except for the one point that the West Avon unlike the East Avon springs not from the chalk but from the greensand which underlies it at the foot of the downs. The East Avon on the other hand has springs of mainly chalk origin even if they too emanate marginally from greensand.

The Upper Avon therefore, as a result of this mixed greensand and chalk fountain-head, is not a true chalk stream, although for all its course as far as Salisbury and beyond it flows through down country, with solid chalk close to either bank. No doubt, too, there are many chalk stream springs in the river bed, which serve to increase its flow. The only effect of this partly greensand origin is to make the headwaters less alkaline than they would be if they came from pure chalk; also the West Avon as a result has a slightly different appearance from that of a true chalk stream, such as the neighbouring Wylye. Indeed, this headwater has something which reminds one more of a small midland brook, winding and with pollarded willows, until close to Upavon where the river soon assumes a true chalk stream character, hardly distinguishable from that of the upper Test or Itchen. All fishing from here downstream as far as Salisbury is classic dry fly water for trout, with grayling in the autumn.

It is in the Upavon area that the main fishing on the upper Avon begins. The East Chisenbury Fishing Syndicate has about three miles of water here on both banks, as far downstream as Enford, well managed and well stocked with trout. This beat produces anything up to seven hundred brown trout in a season, their average weight being around 14 oz. Below this lies the well-known water of The Services Dry Fly Fishing Association, with which the late Frank Sawyer was so closely associated. The author was privileged to have made his acquaintance over a number of years, and whether it was on the riverside or anywhere else it was always a pleasure to meet him and talk with him. He was a member of Charles Ritz's Fario Club in Paris, and frequently attended the annual dinner there, receiving a warm welcome from anglers from all over Europe and America. He was a true countryman, and full of the lore of the riverside, as his book *Keeper of the Stream* bears eloquent testimony. Tall and spare in figure, he was ever careful of words, and never spoke idly or

The Upper Avon above Amesbury, perfect dry fly water

without due consideration. What he said was always worth attention. He was born at the Old Mill House at Bulford in Wiltshire on the upper Avon, and he spent almost all his life keepering on this river, since his first job at the age of eighteen. He was an outstanding Avon figure, and his death in recent years left a sad gap, not only at Netheravon, but in trout fishing circles everywhere.

Another famous character who used often to fish this water was the late Oliver Kite, expert angler and author. He was originally a pupil of Frank Sawyer; and among his various works were *Nymph Fishing in Practice*, and *Fisherman's Diary*. He too was most knowledgeable about all river matters.

The Services Dry Fly Fishing Association water extends on both banks as far downstream as Bulford, three miles short of Amesbury. It provides what is some of the best fishing on the upper Avon, and the Association is indeed fortunate to have at its disposal some six and a half miles of river, well keepered and well managed. The annual bag on this water is of 1,200 or more keepable trout, with a number of grayling also. This Association, first established in the early 1900s, has at present 100 rods drawn from all ranks in all three Services. First priority is given to those serving, then to retired regulars, and next to members of the Reserve Forces. Needless to say there is a long waiting list of applicants for rods.

By the time it reaches Bulford, about fifteen miles from its source, the Avon has grown into a fair sized river, fifteen to twenty yards wide on average, about the size of, say, the Itchen at Chilland or the Test at Wherwell; and who could want better? It has passed through some lovely and typical Wiltshire countryside. To the east and west of its valley lies what would originally have been the down-land of Salisbury Plain, and although this is now mainly cultivated, large areas of it still remain untouched where the Army has extensive training grounds. The main villages on this part of the Avon's course are Upavon, Enford, Netheravon, Figheldean, Durrington and Bulford, all full of charm in their quiet way. Below Bulford the river soon approaches Amesbury. The Salisbury Angling Club has a short stretch of fishing at Totterdown, also a longer stretch at Ratfyn and again at West Amesbury.

On the outskirts of Amesbury the Avon passes through the grounds of Amesbury Abbey, and skirts the ancient township where the former main roads from London to the South West and from Southampton to Bristol and Gloucester cross. A brief digression about the history of such a notable Avon foundation may perhaps be of interest.

Amesbury must for certain have originally been one of the earliest human settlements in the Avon valley. Being so close to ancient centres of worship such as Stonehenge and Woodhenge, it is likely that a village existed here as far back as neolithic times, perhaps in 2000 BC or earlier. The river would have provided both a water supply and means of drainage.

Three miles to the west of Amesbury, and close to the main road to Warminster, lies the prehistoric Bronze Age site of Stonehenge, its largest standing stone having a height of 21 feet. The oldest part of Stonehenge is thought to have been constructed about 1800 BC and the whole structure completed about 1400 BC. This amazing relic of an age long past is thought to have had a religious purpose in connection with sun worship. The method by which the massive blocks of stone were transported to this site and their original place of origin is still uncertain; but it is reckoned that the bluestones forming the inner horseshoe were probably brought in the first place from the Prescelly Hills in Pembrokeshire, a distance of 200 miles, and the sarsen stones in the outer ring from the Marlborough Downs, closer at hand.

Together with Glastonbury Abbey, Amesbury is reputed to have been one of the earliest centres of Christianity in Roman Britain. The name is probably a corruption of 'Ambrosebury', (i.e. Ambrose's town or burial place), Ambrosius Aurelianus being a Romano-British hero of the immediate post-Roman period, who was by legend both born and buried here. Ambrose was said to have been the successful leader during his lifetime of the British forces against the persistent pressure of our main ancestors, the invading Anglo-Saxons; though the written history of the fifth and sixth centuries, the Dark Ages, is both scarce and scattered. He was also the predecessor of King Arthur, another great hero-figure of the age, about whom tantalizingly little reliable information is available. An eighth century British chronicler, Nennius, recorded that Arthur was the victor at the great battle of Mount Badon sometime in the late fifth or early sixth century, where the invading Saxons were decisively beaten. Mount Badon was most probably Badbury Rings, the ancient fortification near Wimborne in Dorset, which the author can see from his window as he writes. This was said to be Arthur's twelfth and greatest victory over the Saxons, and their further influx was held up for a generation or more. Nennius however described Arthur not as a 'King', but as a 'Leader in Battles.' The historian William of Malmesbury writing later, in the early twelfth century, re-echoed Nennius' words in describing Ambrose as 'King of the Britons', and Arthur as his great general. So there may be some doubt as to whether Arthur could properly be described as a 'King' at all. There is no doubt however that Arthur's wife, Guinevere, (described in Welsh legend, incidentally, as 'bad when little, worse when great'), took the veil at the convent of Amesbury; so there must have been a nunnery here as early as the sixth century. Guinevere seems to have led a troubled life, and exercised a disruptive influence in her relations with her paramour, Sir Lancelot, as in other ways. Let us hope she found eventual peace here, after Arthur's death, on the banks of the quietly flowing Avon and amid the rolling Wiltshire downlands. Legend has it that at her death she was 'floated down the river', not in the same fashion as Ophelia but doubtless in some form of stately funeral barge.

Amesbury fell in due course to the invading Saxons, and was probably destroyed; though subsequently there must have been a Saxon church here, as carved Saxon stones have been found on the site of the present church. We learn that in 875 AD King Alfred the Great made a gift of the Amesbury manors to his third son, and this gift carried with it the obligation of the inhabitants to afford shelter and hospitality to the King and his train whenever he passed by. Apart from the church, Queen Ethelfrida the wife of the Saxon King Edgar built a convent here in 980, in expiation of the murder of her step-son Edward the Martyr at Corfe Castle two years earlier. A town soon grew around the convent, and in this guise Amesbury emerged by degrees into the Middle Ages. Royal ladies seem always to have had a predilection for this site—not only Guinevere and Ethelfrida, but in later years Eleanor of Provence, the widow of King Henry III, died here at Amesbury and was buried before the high altar at the Nunnery church. The daughter of King Edward I subsequently became a nun here; also Catherine of Aragon, the daughter of Ferdinand and Isabella of Spain, lodged here in 1501 on her arrival in England to marry first Prince Arthur, the eldest son of King Henry VII, and later his younger brother, King Henry VIII.

Except for a break of two years in 1177, the convent at Amesbury flourished until King Henry VIII's time and his dissolution of the monasteries in 1530; when like so many other similar institutions all over England it was, tragically no doubt, 'dissolved', and its assets sequestrated by the Crown.

Amesbury Abbey, now a place of retirement for the elderly

The Avon at Amesbury Abbey

Amesbury Abbey, the mansion house on the banks of the Avon, is a noble building, still in excellent order. It was originally the residence of the Dukes of Queensbury, leaders in 18th century London of the witty literary and political world, and later since 1824 of the Antrobus family, who hailed formerly from Cheshire. Designed by Inigo Jones (1572–1621), architect and artist, it was rebuilt in 1840 in its present form. It now serves a meritorious purpose as a place of retirement for the elderly.

Amesbury church (of St. Mary and the Cornish St. Melor), with its Norman nave and squat but massive central tower, has been restored too often in the past two centuries to be of much architectural interest. It does, however, possess a Norman font of Purbeck marble; also fragments of thirteenth century glass and a fifteenth century screen.

The present population of Amesbury is around six thousand. It has no industrial output (though it formerly had a great reputation for the manufacture of clay pipes!). It has been characterized as a 'small downland capital', restful and unchanging, which is no doubt a fair description. Its tranquillity of late years has, however, been considerably disturbed by the noisy activity of planes from the nearby Boscombe Down airfield—an inevitable discordant feature of modern life in the countryside anywhere near an air-base or air-port. There is no remedy for this and it has to be endured.

Leaving Amesbury, the Avon follows a generally southerly course through the open rolling Wiltshire countryside of chalk downland studded with beech clumps, and now to a large extent cultivated, towards Salisbury, the metropolis of the Plain. In the ten miles of water between Amesbury and Salisbury lies what is perhaps the best trout fishing on the whole river. Here is the Lake fishing, rented by the Piscatorial Society, as is the opposite bank at Durnford. Below this lies the three and a half miles of Heale fishing, meticulously cared for, well stocked, and well keepered. Heale House, a handsome building, stands in the middle of an outstandingly attractive garden on the banks of the the river. This house sheltered Charles II on his flight back to France after the crushing defeat at Worcester in 1651.

Heale House, from across the Avon

Was Charles in truth a Stuart at all? Some eminent authorities have cast doubts upon this. He was unusually tall, dark, and swarthy. Half French, extremely clever, and a secret Roman Catholic as well as in the end being Louis XIV's pensioner, he managed to maintain his position on the throne, though in his later years he lost the support of a substantial section of the nation. His brother King James II flew the Stuart colours in far more characteristic style, and as an inevitable result was forced to flee the country within three years of his accession. So passed the last of the Stuart kings, and the nation was well rid of them.

Below Heale is the Little Durnford water, rented by the Salisbury Angling Club, which extends right to Old Sarum. All this is delightful water, providing first class fishing. The river by now is bigger, about the size of the Test at Stockbridge or the Itchen at Winchester. Its banks are well cared for as is its weed growth, there being three well regulated weed cuts annually, in early May (when needed), in late June and early July, also during late August. These weed cutting periods apply to all the Avon and its tributaries. Owners on the upper river in this way are able to use their discrimination in weed cutting, both as to the amount and the type of weed which they cut. The cut weed is allowed to float downriver, and the Wessex Water Authority inserts a boom below Salisbury, where it is collected and abstracted, so as to avoid nuisance to anglers further downstream. This system now works well.

Major D. A. C. Rasch in control of his weed-cutting boat at Heale

There are on the Avon, as elsewhere on the chalk rivers, a number of hatches, kept wide open in winter and spring, though partially closed from May onwards to maintain a reasonable head of water. Modern anglers may well be grateful for the legacy of the mediaeval use of water power for mills, also in later times for the system of water meadow irrigation. Mill hatches or irrigation hatches, which were originally totally unassociated with fishing, are an essential attribute to the well being of any chalk stream fishery. To appreciate this, one only has to look to see what happens on a stretch of water where hatches have broken down or been removed, such situations being not altogether uncommon in these days, sad to say. The disastrous situation arising during dry summer weather, or during much of the year for that matter, is apt to become only too apparent. The stream, down to a small proportion of its winter flow, becomes sad

Good mayfly water on the Avon near Lower Woodford

and shrivelled, sometimes trickling only a few inches deep over a semi-dehydrated river bed, largely choked with dying weed. A depressing sight, and goodbye in most places in it to anything but fingerling trout!

All chalk stream anglers should therefore be grateful for frequently recurring hatches, which provide a fair head of water for a substantial distance upstream, and also intriguing hatch pools, where the inflowing water becomes well oxygenated, and which afford a deep and secluded refuge for fish. Few people can walk past a hatch pool without stopping to peer into its depths, and attempting to probe the mystery of what it holds. All sorts of surprises are apt to come to light in such pools. Here is where the monster trout often gather, where they are concealed by the rush of water overhead, and where they find sufficient depth to make them feel secure. Here, too, their food supply descending from upstream is concentrated and easily obtainable, and there are probably back-streams under one or both banks, which provide a further convenient resting place for fish of all sizes.

Here too may be found pike, small or large, where there is a still backwater out of the current where they can rest (they dislike streams). Possibly even a salmon may be found, if it has penetrated thus far upstream, and has paused before attempting to thrust its way through the hatch. Eel stages too are often to be found at hatch pools, though seldom worked at any time except on moonless autumn nights or after heavy rain. But even without all this, the hatch pool seems to induce something approaching a mesmeric effect—the downward rush of water, the concealed depths, the shallowing tail and run-out, and the back currents under either bank, all exercise fascination and merit a long protracted examination.

A word here on the water meadow system, mentioned above. Most of us are familiar with the abundant carriers and 'drawns', together with the small footbridges and side hatches, broken down or other-wise, which are so characteristic of the water meadows alongside our chalk streams and rivers. All these, usually now in a derelict state, are relics of an elaborate irrigation system, largely introduced into England by Dutch engineers in the mid-seventeenth century, when sheep and the wool trade were such important factors in English agriculture.

The object was to gain the ability by the manipulation of hatches to flood the meadows at will, and equally to shut off the water when desired by closing down the inlet hatches and allowing the meadows to run dry as the water drained away from them. By doing this the grass and hay crop was greatly encouraged, being protected from frost if the meadows were 'drowned' in winter or spring, or from drought in summer; the water being turned on or off as wanted. The river and its branches would be manipulated into a high water channel and a low water channel respectively to achieve this object, running parallel though possibly at some little distance apart; and there would be innumerable smaller channels distributing water all over the meadows when they were 'drowned'. Special farm labourers, known as 'drowners', were employed to manage this whole system; but unfortunately it entailed considerable labour and maintenance, carriers and 'drawns' had to be kept unblocked by weed or grass, banks, hatches, and bridges kept repaired, new channels dug from time to time, and other works carried out which entailed constant attention. The result in these latter days of more costly labour has been that the system has almost everywhere been abandoned, and water meadows have been left, as is only too apparent, to look after themselves. Just occasionally in one or two places they are still worked, for instance on the Avon at Heale, Britford, and Somerley; but as a rule it comes as a surprise to see them so. From the fishing point of view this is a loss. Water meadows in use gave extra fishing up the main 'drawns' and carriers, which has been much reduced now they are no longer worked. They also provided an extra reservoir for insect and crustacean food-life for trout. On the other hand, trout sometimes permeated, when meadows were 'drowned', into impossible temporary streams, where they were landlocked when the water was turned off; and if not removed and returned to the main river, were either left high and dry, or else became a prey for poachers or vermin. But this was no real drawback, as it could easily be countered by energetic and watchful fishery management. In addition water meadows, when the stream was percolating through them, acted as a valuable filter whenever the river for any reason was coloured. On balance the demise of the water meadow system is to be greatly regretted.

Trout on the Upper Avon

As previously mentioned, the Upper Avon provides classic trout water. All dry fly fishing, as on the upper Avon, is basically dependent on fly life and the fly hatch. Without fly, or with very little, the fishing fails. The upper Avon, fortunately, is well endowed in this respect, due in turn to prolific weed growth with plenty of ranunculus, a clear gravel bottom varied in places with silt, and absence of pollution in all but minimal amounts. (Where this occasionally occurs, it is mainly due to farm sewage and insecticide spray). Flannel weed, ribbon weed, and 'cat's tails' do of course occur in places, particularly downstream of Amesbury. Their presence is unwelcome, but apart from rigorous cutting and raking there is little that can be done to check their growth. Starwort is also undesirable in anything but fairly small quantities. If allowed to grow too thickly, it checks the stream and harbours silt or mud, (though it does provide a bountiful refuge for fresh-water crustaceans, a valuable form of trout food.) In general however the Avon's weed growth is a healthy one.

The mayfly hatch, so far as fly life is concerned, is the main feature of the season. There has always been a hatch of this kind on some part of the Avon, and in present times it is more than usually prolific. Mayfly abound from about the third week of May onwards, right up to Upavon; and the start of the hatch varies only by a few days, according the occurence of an early or late season. After the main hatch during the last two weeks of May and the first week of June, mayfly become thinned out, and the trout are apt to lose interest in them; but odd specimens appear throughout June and even into August or September. Though on the upper Avon, as mentioned above, the mayfly hatch has been consistent in late years, in some chalk stream areas particularly in headwaters it varies in an inexplicable way. For a period of time on a given stretch of river mayfly may be abundant, and then for no apparent reason may virtually disappear for a further period before reappearing again. It is hard to see why this should happen, though high gales at the time of the

Upper Avon, looking downstream from Amesbury Bridge

hatch may be a possible contributory cause, if they blow the imago far away from the river so that reproduction fails. At Heale for example during the twenty years 1960–1980 there was no mayfly at all. Now it proliferates there.

In any case, whether the presence of mayfly is an advantage or not from the fishing angle is a permanent point of dispute amongst dry fly men. On the one hand this hatch provides a good chance of luring the 3 and 4 pounders which seldom rise to other types of fly. It provides a happy opportunity for beginners and the inexperienced of catching something really worth while, as trout often rise so freely to mayfly that they are not difficult for even a moderately skilled angler to deceive. Also abundant mayfly helps greatly to bring fish into the pink of condition. At the same time though, after some preliminary hesitation during the first day or two of the hatch, there is no doubt that trout become satiated on a rich diet of mayfly; and for two or three weeks after mayfly time they become reluctant to rise to any other form of fly. June and early July are therefore often dull months on mayfly waters, and at this period of the midsummer late evening fishing is probably the most rewarding, just as the light begins to fail. So it cuts both ways, and it can be argued that absence or comparative absence of mayfly produces free-er rising fish during the summer months. Other types of fly such as olives (including the B.W.O.), iron blues, and pale wateries are reasonably plentiful. The only time when the fly hatch seems sparse is the daytime of the mid-summer weeks, a fairly general characteristic everywhere in this part of the world.

The upper Avon water is alkaline in content, as are all chalk streams, perhaps less so than normal in its uppermost reaches owing to its West Avon greensand origin, but nevertheless on a scale sufficient to support a large population of freshwater shrimp and snails. Although these detract from the trouts' penchant for the floating fly, they do provide a most valuable source of food, and it is crustaceans such as these that produce that delicious pink flesh in the cooked trout which is so highly prized. Crayfish too used to be plentiful, until that disastrous disease which started in the Avon headwaters a year or two ago. This is something of a catastrophe, as this disease is wholly fatal and is carried downstream quickly. At the time of writing it reported to have reached the Fordingbridge area, some 13 miles below Salisbury, and to be spreading although much more slowly up the tributaries such as the Wylye and Nadder. So it appears the crayfish in the Avon catchment area are doomed, a sad loss to the trout's menu in the case of the smaller specimens. One can only hope that this disease does not spread into other river areas.

One thing which chalk streams such as the upper Avon are spared is sudden rises of water, such as the spates of north country hill rivers which can cause so much damage to banks and river beds. After heavy rains the Avon naturally rises, but in a much slower fashion, giving ample warning of its intention. Equally it can retain its height for long periods at a time—no river ever falls as quickly as it rises.

But even when the springs have welled to full capacity, or after melted snow, the upper river seldom overtops its banks and spreads out into its water meadows. It is more inclined to do this, as a matter of fact, in its lower reaches below Salisbury or near Ringwood, where occasionally one has seen water meadows in February and March resembling a lake—a state of affairs beloved by geese, swans, gulls and waterfowl of all sorts.

Even if in the upper river surplus water does permeate in time of flood into the meadows, little direct damage is done to trout. These normally have time with the slowly falling flood level to find their way back into the main river or its carriers, if in fact they have strayed from them, (though it is worth a look around after a spell of high water to see if any have become isolated; if so it is not difficult to capture and return them to a main channel).

Banks both of main river and carriers are nevertheless likely to suffer limited damage from floods, and they can also be harmed by cattle forming drinking places, and by the excavations of water voles. A periodic inspection is always worthwhile, and repairs should be effected without delay while damage is still small. If not, every succeeding flood will make it worse, and the eventual and inevitable repair will become ever more onerous and expensive. Loose chalk, well packed, is the best repair material; though willow cuttings and brushwood well pegged down, and rammed tight with a layer of earth seeded with grass on top of it, may be nearly as good, and more easily transported. Piling along the water edge may also be necessary, elm, larch, or ash stakes providing the best material. It is often said that river flows have lately decreased. This is not proven. One reason for the apparent lack of flow is the increased width of the river bed, due to banks not being revetted and maintained.

Trees along the bank edge have advantages. They provide shelter from wind and bright sun, and their roots form a valuable strengthening for banks that otherwise might wear away. Occasionally caterpillars or grubs or other forms of trout food may fall off their branches into the water. But such trees should not be too thick or too frequent, so as to keep the water in perpetual shade. If they are allowed to become so, no weed will grow in the river there without sunlight, in the same way as no undergrowth will be found elsewhere under the shade of thick beech trees. Such a shaded stretch of river will become barren and deserted.

Water meadows border the Avon near Lower Woodford

On the upper Avon, as on most other chalk streams, the question of stocking has become a consideration of the first importance. Whether stocking should be embarked upon or not, and if so to what extent it should be done, depends entirely on the expected intensity of the fishing. A mile or so of river of the size and capacity of the upper Avon might reasonably be expected to produce thirty to forty wild trout each year of 1 lb or over, provided there is adequate spawning ground and the vermin is kept down, (pike are the worst). If however a considerably larger bag is required to keep a number of rods happy on such a stretch of river, as seems often to be the case in present times, resort will inevitably have to be made to stocking. There comes a point when, even with the most skilful keepering, wild trout will be unable to provide the numbers that are required.

There are several different methods of stocking. The first is to buy healthy trout from a fish farm, three year olds of say 13 to 16 inches in length with perhaps some larger specimens amongst them, and turn in a suitable number of these at the start and perhaps again at the middle of the season. Fish of this type are easily caught, and as many as possible should be killed during the current year. They are unlikely to do well in their new wild surroundings, and by the following season will probably have disappeared, or else have deteriorated in condition. Although this system gives immediate returns, it is open to obvious drawbacks, and gives an unavoidable aura of artificiality to the fishing. It may however be unavoidable, or partially so.

The second method is to turn in during the spring two year old trout of around 10 inches in length, and to ensure that if caught they are returned to the water during the first season. This system works reasonably well in that by the following year such fish will have grown to a keepable size of 1 lb or over, and will have assumed much of the outlook and semblance of wild trout. They will not by then be so easy to catch, and should have found out how to look after themselves in their wild state. They will also still be at the stage of natural quick growth, and if the food in the river is plentiful, as it should be, they will put on weight. The drawback to this system is of course that during the course of the full year, (and it is necessary to give such fish the benefit of a full summer's feeding) a number of such two year olds will spread out of the fishery either upstream or downstream, or will be lost in other ways. This loss has inevitably to be taken into account, though it helps if upstream and downstream neighbours stock in a similar way.

A third method is to put in large numbers of small yearling trout or fry. Though this would seem basically to be a sound method, because such fish will eventually develop all the characteristics of the wild trout, it will be at least two years before any return in keep-able fish can be expected from them; and during that time the loss from all causes will be massive. Such small fish have their best chance if introduced in small side streams or carriers, where pike and large trout (themselves predators) seldom penetrate. This method, although it may be the least costly, in the end probably produces the smallest return.

Consideration should also be given to the size of the river in question. It is a sound principle never to stock with fish larger than the naturally grown wild trout of equivalent age that it holds. For instance it is obviously misplaced to introduce 2 and 3 pounders into a small stream where in the normal course of events a 1 lb fish is a good one. Such artificially reared large fish are bound to deteriorate rapidly and to be nothing but an incubus in water that is totally unsuited to hold them.

So which is the best method of stocking? Consideration should be given to all three, and perhaps a judicious mixture of all of them may well be the best possible answer. Expense will also have to be taken into account, especially when stock fish have to be bought from a fish farm. A fishery owner who has good fish stews and can rear his own fish from the fry stage naturally has an advantage here.

Whether stocking takes place or not, it is essential that vermin in a chalkstream should be kept down to the lowest possible level. In all but headwaters pike are the worst intruders. They exert a per-petual toll on trout stocks, and unending war should be waged against them. The pike is so streamlined in shape that for a short distance he can make a rush outspeeding any trout, and even if he misses his prey on one occasion he will quickly succeed on another. Electric fishing with a D.C. machine is undoubtedly the best way of dealing with pike—alternating current has too severe an effect on the resident trout. Once a year is enough for this treatment in order to avoid excessive shocking of trout, and there is no better way of keeping pike down. Even so one can never eliminate them completely, and they are always apt to creep in from neighbouring waters; but this method of control is undoubtedly far better than that of netting which it has superseded. It is however sometimes useful to use a stop net in combination with an electric fishing machine, particularly in order to round up large shoals of grayling or coarse fish.

Another effective method of catching pike is through the use of large wire cagetraps. Set in backwaters or in the slack of stagnant holes beloved by pike, these cagetraps are very useful. Always set and always fishing they exert a steady toll on any pike that may be present. It helps if they are partially covered with weed, which makes them look more natural, and if a sizeable unspawned female pike is caught in March, April or May, it pays to leave her alive in the trap for some time, as she will certainly draw in male pike after her. The traps however should be inspected daily, as trout often enter them and these should be released before they injure themselves. Coarse fish also enter these traps occasionally, but grayling never.

Pike spawn in April or soon afterwards, and to do this they often enter shallow carriers and side streams. If found there it is not difficult to deal with them. Fortunately pike seldom ascend to the highest reaches of chalk streams, and they seem to dislike the colder and more highly oxygenated water nearer the springs. Why this should be so is not known for certain, but it has been suggested that their spawn will not hatch in such water. They definitely prefer the slacker backwaters or side streams of the middle and lower reaches, which is where they should be looked for; and they dislike shallow and streamy water.

Grayling are frequent inhabitants of chalk streams, such as the upper Avon. Although some fishermen tolerate them for the sake of autumn and winter fishing, they are normally classed as vermin, and if present in too great numbers they crowd the trout out and eat a disproportionate amount of the available food supply. They are better removed, and again there is no more effective way of doing this than by electric D.C. fishing. Nevertheless they are extremely prolific and it is difficult to keep their numbers down. At Heale and Lake for instance, two famous fisheries on the Avon above Salisbury, the catch of grayling every year by electric fishing approaches 2,000 and such numbers continually recur, season after season. During 1985 for instance, no less than 1,200 grayling were removed from the Heale water by electric fishing. One wonders what levels their numbers would reach if they were not kept down in this way!

Coarse fish, such as chub, roach, and dace are only a minor problem on this part of the river, though in the Salisbury area and below they are encouraged by coarse fishermen. Eels are always present, though their numbers can be substantially reduced by electric fishing. It is difficult to assess the amount of damage which they do. They are present in all chalk rivers, as well as in other waters, and no doubt devour quantities of sub-surface food which would otherwise be available for trout. How far they prey on ova, alevin, fry and yearling trout is impossible to estimate. One would have thought little on ova, as they are usually hibernating at spawning time if they have not already left for the sea. But at other stages of development trout must be at risk from them.

Eels are unpleasant creatures and so far as one knows do no good, except possibly as scavengers. Eel stages or weirs are of little use in reducing their numbers, as their catch is mainly of mature eels returning to the sea, which are on the point of disappearing in any case. Electric fishing is perhaps the best way of keeping them down.

Herons are a permanent hazard, particularly in the spawning season. They will spear anything that moves within their reach, and are particularly hard on spawning trout, which seem to lose their sense of self-preservation at that time, and enter ludicrously shallow water. If the fish is too large for the heron to swallow it whole or lift it out of the water, that does not stop him spearing it. Sizeable trout can sometimes be found lying on the bank with a hole through them, made by the heron's bill; it is the lower mandible incidentally, which the heron uses for stabbing, and he appears to strike with his beak open. Sometimes too one discovers a stabbed trout, which has escaped and survived—the wound having healed—but he is likely to be in poor condition in this state.

Other birds can be a nuisance. Swans if too plentiful can disturb the water, stripping away the weed, and at nesting time dispute the banks. They should be discouraged. Cormorants have no redeeming features. No effort should be spared to discourage them. Fortunately these seldom ascend to the upper stretches of chalk rivers, and are much more plentiful lower down. They are ugly birds, wholly fish-eaters, and totally unwelcome. Being strong underwater swimmers, no fish of a size small enough for them to swallow can escape them.

Gulls often penetrate far inland, but do little or no harm apart from eating a certain amount of fly and the odd fingerling trout. King-fishers, if present, are wholly delightful. They do very little harm except on fry ponds, but can easily be kept out of these by fine mesh netting.

To sum up there is delightful dry fly fishing on the upper Avon, and nymph fishing is allowed under certain conditions on some stretches. As on other neighbouring chalk rivers, if the angler is looking for sport, pleasure, and scenic beauty, he would have to travel very far afield from here to find its like.

4 lbs 2 ozs wild brown trout caught at Heale on dry fly in 1935

Old Sarum and New Sarum

The upper Avon's course and its fishing has now been traced as far as Little Durnford, and so to Old Sarum, and New Sarum or the modern Salisbury. Some account of the history of both these famous foundations follows.

About one mile downstream of Little Durnford, the Avon skirts on its left bank the three hundred feet high projecting spur of Salisbury Plain, whereon is situated Old Sarum—a remarkable relic of Roman, Saxon and Norman occupations. This site also no doubt dates back to neolithic times, as does that of Amesbury, and it is older than the present city of Salisbury by well over a thousand years of recorded history. In Roman times, Old Sarum was certainly a garrison stronghold, known as Sorbiodunum. It was never a township on the scale of Winchester, Silchester, or Dorchester, but nevertheless was a provincial centre of considerable local significance.

After the departure of the Roman legions in the early fifth century, Old Sarum finally fell to the invading Saxons in 552 AD (according to the Saxon Chronicle). They renamed it Sarisbyrig, and it continued to feature as a place of local importance throughout the Saxon era. During the time of the Danish invasions it changed hands between Saxons and Danes on more than one occasion, until it was finally sacked and burnt by the Danish King Sweyn in 1003. But this was by no means the end of its story. The savage Norman military occupation of the country after 1066 ensured that a 'motte and bailey' castle, comprising ditch, ramparts and keep, was erected on this prominent position, which dominated the surrounding countryside. Norman remains have been found in profusion at Old Sarum, and in addition to the castle with its earldom, a cathedral with its bishop was also set up here. A township, renamed Salisberie, grew up once again around these foundations, and four mills are recorded in the Domesday Book along the Avon in this area. The name 'Sarum', incidentally, appears to owe its origin to a clerk's abbreviation at about this time, which was copied and eventually adopted.

In 1174 the Castle of Old Sarum was used by King Henry II for

Old Sarum from across the Avon

ten years, until her release in 1184, as a place of confinement for his Queen, the redoubtable Eleanor of Aquitaine. This lady previous to her marriage with Henry had been the wife of King Louis VII of France until the annulment of their marriage. She must have been a formidable character, witness the advice given to Louis by his barons: 'I'faith the best counsel that we can give you is that ye let her go; for she is a very devil, and if ye keep her long we fear that she will cause you to be murdered.'

In addition to being firstly Queen of France and subsequently Queen of England, Eleanor was in her own right the hereditary Duchess of Aquitaine and sovereign over a large part of what is now France, including Poitou and all provinces south of the Loire, among them Saintonge, Limousin, Guienne, and Gascony. She was also the mother of two famous Kings of England, Richard I (Coeur de Lion), and his younger brother John. No doubt it needed a strong castle such as that of Old Sarum to keep such a forceful lady captive.

Shortly afterwards the history of 'New Sarum', the present city of Salisbury, as opposed to 'Old Sarum', begins. The dual control of Old Sarum by earl and bishop in the Norman era and early Plantagenet era led to trouble, as dual controls often do. In addition, the clergy of Old Sarum complained that 'being in a raised place the continued gusts of wind make such a noise that the clerks can hardly hear one another sing, and the place is so rheumatic by reason of the wind that they often suffer in health'. Besides this, the water supply by well proved insufficient for garrison, clergy and townsfolk. The result was that the clergy and townsfolk, under the aegis of Bishop Richard Poore, about the the year 1226, in the words of the chronicler, 'descended to the plain'; i.e. they deserted Old Sarum, lock stock and barrel, and moved two miles down to the area of the present Cathedral Close, to found there a new Cathedral and a new township near to where the waters of the Avon and Nadder meet. So the foundation of the present city of Salisbury, although it dates far enough back, does not compare in antiquity with that of neighbouring townships such as Wilton and Amesbury.

The planning of the new Cathedral was then begun; and the construction of it, though not yet completed, was sufficiently advanced by 1258 for it to be consecrated. In 1334 work was started on the magnificent spire, 404 feet high and the highest in Europe after that of Ulm, its completion taking the best part of thirty years. This spire is a notable landmark for the whole neighbourhood, being clearly visible at twelve miles distance, if no rise of downland intervenes. When one regards the whole of this remarkable edifice one is given to wondering how the architects and builders of the early Middle Ages, with their somewhat primitive implements and methods, and without the aid of machinery, could have possibly produced such an amazing constructional masterpiece. Then one remembers that buildings such as the Parthenon and the Colosseum were built a thousand or more years earlier, so perhaps it is not such a miracle after all. Incidentally, two other interesting details are that New Sarum or Salisbury, as it came to be called, possesses the only medieval cathedral in the country to remain architecturally exactly as it was originally planned and without any subsequent additions over the centuries; also that this cathedral houses what is claimed to be the oldest clock in Britain, dating from 1386. This 'clock' is an amazing conglomeration of cogwheels, weights, pulleys and cords, which is still in working order. It has no hands, but merely strikes the hours.

Externally, Salisbury Cathedral is of course a marvel. Internally it is not so impressive, and does not compare, for instance, with Winchester Cathedral or Westminster Abbey; but how far this may be due to depredations committed during the Reformation and Commonwealth is open to question. Certainly, apart from any consideration of architecture, the setting of the Cathedral when viewed from any angle, but particularly across the Avon as immortalized by Constable, is beyond compare.

As a matter of interest, it has recently been calculated that the 6,400 tons of stone in the tower and spire exerts a pressure of 20 tons per square foot on its flint clay and gravel foundation. It is doubtful whether any modern builder would allow much more than 2 tons per square foot on such a foundation, yet Salisbury spire still stands erect after 650 years. It is indeed a miracle of architecture, and although there have been various alarms about subsidence and variation from the true perpendicular (the tip of the spire is said to be twenty one inches out of the vertical at this present time), nevertheless up to the present neither fire nor weather nor stone falls nor 'improvements' by later architects have impaired its original magnificent appearance. It is now asserted in this year 1985 that the Cathedral and its spire need major reconstruction work. Let us all hope that this work will be successful in preserving both Cathedral and spire for at least a further 650 years.

The city of New Sarum or Salisbury, as it became to be called, was thus almost wholly of ecclesiastical origin, and the great Cathedral grew to dominate the countryside both visually owing to its spire, and episcopally as the centre of a diocese stretching far and wide over Wessex. It was quite separated from Old Sarum by two miles of countryside, and this latter was now deserted except as a military outpost. (Nevertheless, Old Sarum was allotted two seats in

View across the Nadder of Salisbury Cathedral

Parliament by King Edward I and thus became one of the notorious 'rotten boroughs' which were not done away with until the Reform Bill of 1832.)

No doubt the new city's site was chosen with a view to the advantages accruing from the near presence of the Avon, close to its confluence with the Nadder. Salisbury, as it became, has frequently been described as the meeting place of five different rivers, the Avon, Wylye, Nadder, Bourne and Ebble. Broadly speaking this is true, but in detail not, as the Wylye runs first into the Nadder some two miles upstream at Quidhampton, just below Wilton. Only the Nadder actually joins the Avon close to Salisbury; while the Bourne runs in about one mile further downstream, and the Ebble at Bodenham, two miles further down. However, this is to argue about trivialities, and the general sense is clear. The site of New Sarum was described by the contemporary chronicler as possessing 'rich fields and fertile valleys, abounding in the fruits of the earth and watered by living streams'.

One special feature of interest is that in early mediaeval times it was possible for sea-going 'ships' to pass up the Avon from its mouth at Christchurch as far as Salisbury. In fact, since the Act of Parliament in 1644, the Avon is still classed as a 'navigable river' as far as Salisbury, though sandbanks by the above date had largely choked the entrance to Christchurch harbour. One wonders how mediaeval 'ships' were propelled against the river's current, whether by oar, pole, or sail, or towed from the bank. It must have demanded considerable effort. Of course, such ships were small, probably no bigger than moderate sized modern barges. They would also have been dependent on a fair height of water in the river to enable them to clear the shallow stretches. Their passage upstream would also have ruled out the possibility of mills and hatches on the lower river, since locks have never existed on the Avon at any time. It also seems that this must have occurred before the construction of the bridges at Fordingbridge and Ringwood, as the clearance afforded by their arches is insufficient for little more than a row boat.

The passage of such 'ships' is, however, an indication of how important rivers were in mediaeval times in providing an avenue for transport, both from the coast upriver, and from inland areas down to the sea. Wheeled transport was then rudimentary and unreliable, and roads were primitive. Pack animals could carry only a limited load. Water transport provided a ready to hand and more efficient alternative. It is interesting to note that, however far-fetched it may seem to describe the Salisbury of that age as a 'port', the city nevertheless fulfilled the obligations of a port of the time in providing and manning a ship, the 'Trout', during the Hundred Years War, which helped to protect the coast of Kent and Sussex from a possible French invasion.

Apart from the Cathedral, Salisbury contains many fine old buildings around the Close and in the area of Crane Street, some dating back to the 13th century. The Bishop's Palace and the Deanery are outstanding amongst them, also Mompesson House, built much later in 1701 for the family of that name. The Close is surrounded by a wall built under licence from King Edward III (1327–1377), which still stands.

In the Cathedral cloisters is the library built in 1445, which contains many ancient manuscripts, including a page of the Old Testament in Latin dating back to the 8th century, and most famous of all a copy of Magna Carta, one of the four contemporary copies still in existence.

Harnham Bridge

There is an ancient bridge on the outskirts of Salisbury, Harnham Bridge over the Avon, which was originally built in King Henry III's reign (1216–1272), and is still in use. One wonders how the mediaeval citizens contrived otherwise to cross the many river branches. No doubt it was possible to ford them in places during the summer, though not in winter. Perhaps in fact there was little need to cross them, except occasionally by ferry boat; or there may have been wooden bridges, long vanished. In any case, the Crane Street bridge also dates back to mediaeval times, and this provided an alternative method of crossing the Avon.

Salisbury continued always to be a prominent local centre in the mediaeval era right into modern times, not only owing to its Cathedral but also as a thriving market town, the natural metropolis of the surrounding area. The royal sanction for the creation of a market was obtained at the same time as the foundation of the city, and this market still exists today. It was, of course, the wool trade, so important an economic factor in mediaeval England, which originally brought Salisbury its wealth; also the cloth trade. The Black Death, in the mid-1300s, no doubt took its toll of the City's inhabitants, but Salisbury survived. It produced archers, infantry, and horses for the Hundred Years War against France. Later, in the time of the Civil War, the City's sympathies lay firmly with Parliament, but fortunately it escaped serious injury through pillage or fighting, apart from some damage to the interior of the Cathedral by Parliament's Puritan troops.

No doubt in later times Salisbury also owed someting to its situation as a principal coaching station between London and the South-West. But the main railway arrived at Salisbury in 1857 and soon put a stop to coaching. Passengers were carried by train to London in four hours (half the time of the fastest possible coach journey), and at a first class return fare of 24/-. Besides this, a separate line to Warminster and Bristol had been opened in 1856. These rail links had the effect of putting Salisbury in far closer touch with the surrounding areas and of giving a stimulus to trade, as well as encouraging an influx of visitors, some of whom moved in permanently.

In modern days, Salisbury has increased greatly in size, and is now a flourishing city of some 35,500 inhabitants. The number of visitors it attracts every year is immense.

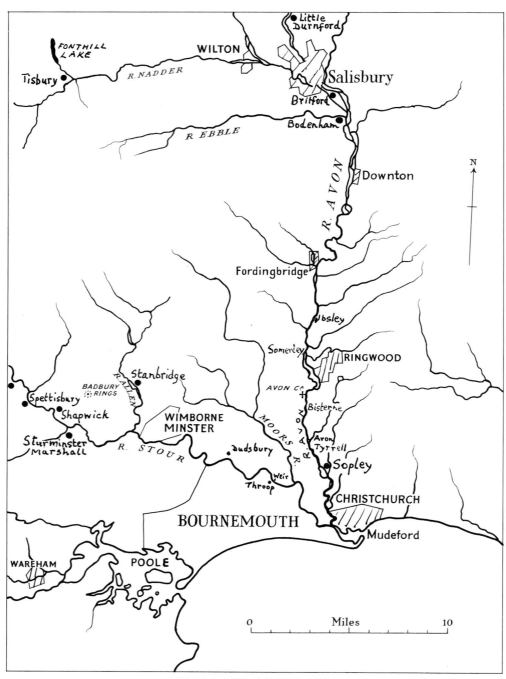

MIDDLE AND LOWER AVON
Showing lower Stour and river Allen

SALISBURY TO THE SEA

(Middle and Lower Avon)

The Middle Avon

To return to the modern Avon and its course, downstream from Old Sarum and Stratford sub Castle through Salisbury city and as far as the Cathedral Close the Salisbury Angling Club still has fishing rights except for one short interval. The main river, leaving the precincts of Salisbury and now doubled in size by the combined flow of the Wylye and Nadder, continues its south-easterly veering southerly course towards Britford (with its Saxon church), Alderbury, and Longford Castle. It is joined in this area by two more sizeable tributaries, the Bourne which runs in from the north-east and meets the main river about a mile below Salisbury, and the Ebble from the west which runs in a further mile and half downstream at Bodenham village immediately below Longford Castle. The main river in the neighbourhood of Longford is divided into three different channels, a legacy no doubt of the water meadow system, each of which provides coarse fish of many varying sorts. Trout too are still reasonably plentiful in this part of the river, doubtless aided by stocking. Some of them run to a large size, but these are seldom caught except on bait or during the mayfly season. Tom Williams, Lord Radnor's fishery manager, in his interesting book *A River for All Seasons* describes the Avon record trout as weighing $16\frac{1}{2}$ lb, caught no doubt by some means other than a dry fly. He also records one of 'just under 10 lb caught on a nymph'. Downstream of Longford however the trout fishing on the Avon soon deteriorates.

Salmon in high water years sometimes arrive in this part of the

45

river in fair numbers, though in low water the Longford beats produce little, as the salmon have difficulty in ascending obstacles further downstream. The Longford fishing continues for a considerable distance, as far as Downton.

From this point onwards, as might be expected after the confluence of five rivers, the main Avon assumes a different character. It becomes much larger and wider, slower flowing with increased silt, increased weed, and less gravel at its bed. It no longer has the character of a delightful trout water, such as that provided by its upper reaches and by tributaries such as Wylye or Nadder. Trout fishing down here is confined mainly to the mayfly time, and coarse fish predominate. In tune with the increased size of the river, the whole valley opens wider, and though still most pleasant in character one feels it has lost the charming seclusion and intimacy of the smaller headwaters above Salisbury.

Longford Castle, mentioned above, and home of the Earls of Radnor, is largely of 16th century origin and is built to a triangular pattern. Like Wilton House it has a magnificent collection of pictures and other works of art, also some lovely gardens.

Trafalgar House, another famous edifice which lies close to the Avon's left bank a further two miles downstream, was built in 1733, and was presented by the nation to Admiral Lord Nelson's family in 1814 in gratitude for His Lordship's services against the French navy, culminating in the great victory after which the house was named. In this house there is a 'Ganges Room', the panelling of which is formed from the timber of H.M.S. Ganges, a man o' war which took part in Nelson's victory at Copenhagen in 1801. Nelson himself of course never survived to take up residence in this house; but at one time his armchair, couch, telescope and cane were all said to be preserved here. His collateral descendants no longer live here, having been forced out through taxation not long ago by an ungrateful government.

From Trafalgar, and passing through Lord Radnor's great trout farm near Standlynch, the largest in the country, the Avon pursues its course southwards until it reaches Downton, a small country town some five miles south of Salisbury. Downton has produced a Roman mosaic pavement, dating back to around 330 AD and now in Salisbury museum, so that its original foundation was obviously a very ancient one. The mediaeval Downton, known as 'The Borough', was built by the Bishop of Winchester around 1205. There was also supposed to have been a mediaeval castle here, built by King John, but all trace of it has disappeared. The modern town is divided in two by the Avon, on the banks of which exists a tannery, still in use. Downton is a renowned coarse fishing centre, also large trout used to be caught in its area during the mayfly time, though nowadays they seem to be scarce.

One and a half miles downstream from Downton the Avon passes out of Wiltshire into Hampshire. It skirts on its right bank at this point the village of Breamore, a delightful and peaceful refuge from the busy modern world. Breamore (like Britford), possesses the rare endowment of a Saxon church, dedicated to St. Mary, and dating from about 1000 AD. Breamore House, belonging to the Hulse family

The Saxon church at Breamore

for over 200 years, was completed in 1583 and has a splendid collection of works of art, furniture, and tapestries. It stands in a commanding position on rising ground, about a mile back from the river.

At Rockbourne, $2\frac{1}{2}$ miles from Breamore, there is a fine example of a Roman villa, or rather of its remains. This appears to have been one of the largest villas in England, with no less than seventy-three rooms, and dating from the second century AD. It held several fine mosaics, and a bath complex with hypocaust. A large museum adjoins the villa, containing coins both silver and bronze, rings and bracelets, brooches, glass, Samian pottery, tools, keys and locks, tiles, stone carvings, dice and counters, all found on this site. Further excavations here are still periodically carried out.

Rockbourne itself is a charming and remote country village, with many thatched Tudor and Georgian cottages and houses. It lies on a small brook, which eventually runs into the Avon.

A further few miles takes the river to Fordingbridge, (pop. 5,000), another small and pleasant country town of ancient foundation. Here

Breamore House

PLATE 2

A hatch pool on the Upper Avon

Typical water on the Upper Avon

PLATE 3

Salisbury—St Thomas's from Crane Bridge

Painted by Paul Stewart

is found the old road bridge with its seven arches, which replaced the original mediaeval fording across the Avon. This bridge was built in the 15th century, and is still in use, though adapted to cater for modern traffic.

All this part of the river was famous for its coarse fishing. Trout fishing downstream of Longford has largely faded out, and salmon fishing except for one small hatch pool at Bickton is of little account above Ibsley, five miles below Fordingbridge. Coarse fishing in this area therefore reigns supreme. Fordingbridge used to be a great coarse fishing centre. There is a well known hotel on the banks of the river here, the Albany, noted for the fishing facilities which it arranged for its guests. Another hotel renowned for its fishing is the Bull at Downton—both of these became gathering places for anglers from all over the country. Coarse fish numbers have now declined (See p. 101).

The Avon in this neighbourhood is continually split into different channels, a result of the water meadow system. But there is no harm in this, as such channels are apt to provide good fishing in their own

The old bridge at Fordingbridge

right, some of the larger carriers being as productive as the main river itself. The extent of the fishing is thereby greatly increased. Specimen fish of many types are to be found in this part of the river, for instance the record Avon pike of $37\frac{1}{2}$ lb was caught close to Fordingbridge in October 1944 (see p. 99).

Moyles Court

One and half miles downstream of Fordingbridge the river flows past and feeds another large trout farm at Bickton, and a further three miles takes it to Ibsley where there is a set of hatches, also a handsome road bridge. Close to Ibsley lies Moyles Court, the scene of a tragedy resulting from Monmouth's rebellion in 1685. Here in those days lived an elderly lady, Lady Alicia Lisle, the widow of one of the regicides of 1649. This lady gave shelter to two fugitives from the Battle of Sedgemoor, and for this crime was hauled before the 'bloody' Judge Jefferies at Winchester Assizes. He condemned her to be burned or beheaded at the King's pleasure, in spite of the bitter indignation of the local Hampshire population. It was the latter sentence which at the insistence of King James II was finally carried out at Winchester, and Lady Alicia's body was escorted by her local supporters all the way to Ellingham church near Ibsley, where she lies buried. One cannot but feel that King James was taking a mean revenge in this case for the beheading of his father, King Charles I, thirty-six years earlier.

Ibsley also marks the beginning of Lord Normanton's Somerley Estate, with fishing on both banks for salmon and coarse fish for the best part of five miles down to Ringwood. There are also two trout lakes here, as well as a trout fishery in a side stream, all of which are kept well stocked. This is one of the pleasantest areas in the whole main Avon valley. Except at one point close to Ibsley the main road is far enough from the river side not to mar the peace and tranquility of the water meadows. All forms of duck and water fowl abound here, and in winter white front geese and Bewick's swans arrive every year in hundreds.

There is a particular lushness about these Avon water meadows, both at Somerley and elsewhere, during May and June, though they are full of interest for that matter during the changing scenes of all the rest of the year. One encounters so many different forms of wildlife—ospreys for instance on rare occasions, and much more frequently Slavonian grebes; herons and cormorants, both fish predators, are common. Occasionally one is lucky enough to catch a glimpse of the sapphire gem of a kingfisher as it darts along the river in rapid flight. Kingfishers as a matter of fact are not rare in southern England, and may be found almost anywhere on its chalk streams or rivers. They are unsociable birds; and the cock bird usually contrives to keep about a quarter of a mile of river as its exclusive domain, driving away even the hen bird except at mating time. They feed on nothing except small forms of fish, and therefore suffer badly during the prolonged frosts of exceptionally cold winters when ice cuts off their food supply. They have one form of unusual protection however, in that they are seldom preyed upon by hawks or other predatory birds, as not surprisingly their flesh is foul tasting to such birds. So far as wild duck are concerned, mallard and wigeon are common, also teal and tufted duck. The following also appear occasionally, pintail, gadwall, pochard, goldeneye, shoveler, goosander, and merganser. The latter two breeds, being exclusively fish eaters, are not welcome to anglers.

Turning to animal life, roe deer abound in the woods and coverts on either bank of the Avon, though they are seldom seen in its water meadows—equally badgers are more common than might be supposed, though being nocturnal in habit they too are seldom seen. Otters were once common, but now seem to have disappeared, which is sad as they are delightful animals. Mink unfortunately are plentiful. They were never indigenous, but all owe their origin in this country to the many mink farms which flourished briefly after the 1939–45 war. Many are trapped every year up and down the lower Avon, but they are prolific and manage to maintain their numbers. They are also voracious, and will destroy any form of bird, animal, or fish life that they can attack. It is probable, for instance, that the present shortage of otters is largely due to mink, as these would be able to enter any otter holt, and would kill the otter cubs if the parents were absent fishing or for other reasons. Unfortunately it is safe to say that, as with other artificially introduced pests such as the grey squirrel, we shall never now be rid of mink. They have already penetrated on the Avon as far upstream as Salisbury, with odd ones further still. They have one merit however, they do kill rats.

Other small animals frequently make their presence known; for instance that harmless creature the water vole can often be seen scuttling or swimming along the river bank; while in spring the apparently mad antics of March hares are a periodic source of entertainment.

Somerley House, belonging to Lord Normanton, is an 18th century building, standing half a mile back from the river on high ground. It has a delightful garden, and is well sited to command a sweeping view down the river towards Ringwood and the New Forest beyond. This house, too, has a magnificent collection of pictures.

On the left bank of the Avon at the bottom of the Somerley water stands Ringwood, a busy market town of around 12,000 inhabitants. Ringwood has always had a strong New Forest connection, though the present Forest boundary lies some two miles away. It is another town of very ancient origin, certainly dating back to Saxon times. The White Hart hotel is perhaps the oldest building in the town, the foundations of which date from the 16th century. It was there that the Duke of Monmouth was lodged under guard after his defeat at Sedgemoor in 1685 and subsequent capture from a hiding place in a ditch near Horton village in Dorset. Poor man, he was en route as a prisoner for London and eventual execution in particularly brutal fashion.

Ringwood is another noted coarse fishing centre, and the Avon here, both upstream and downstream, provides salmon too. In former days there used to be a weir at Ringwood which formed something of an obstacle to the passage of salmon upstream, but twenty five years ago when the main road by-pass was constructed, the bed of the river was artificially shifted for a short distance, and a new weir was built with the inclusion of an efficient and improved salmon ladder, so that ever since that date fish pass upwards with ease.

Old bridge across the Avon at Ringwood

Lower Avon

Two miles below Ringwood the Avon flows past Avon Castle, a tur-
retted building of Victorian type (handsome enough when viewed
from a distance), then past Bisterne, Avon Tyrrell, Sopley, Winkton
and so eventually to Christchurch, with its mouth into the English
Channel at Mudeford.

Bisterne House. Originally built in mediaeval times

Near Bisterne lies the picturesquely named Tyrrell's Ford, which
conjures up in imagination the desperately fugitive Sir Walter Tyrrell
fleeing headlong from the scene of the death in 1100 AD of King
William Rufus in the New Forest—Was this episode an accident or
murder? Obviously Sir Walter was far from easy in mind about it,
to put it mildly, and here forded the Avon, then bridgeless, in his
flight to reach the coast and find himself a ship to take him to Nor-
mandy, which he reached successfully and thus passed out of history.
William Rufus, by all accounts, was a thoroughly evil individual as

well as a deplorable king, and who was England's great benefactor in this affair we shall now never know; but Sir Walter's reckless haste seems significant.

In reaching Mudeford the Avon completes a course of about 70 miles, and drains a catchment area of approximately 658 square miles, compared with that of the Test 446 square miles, and the Frome 190 square miles. Its last sizeable tributary has been the Hampshire Allen (not however to be confused with the Stour's Dorset Allen,) which runs in on its right bank at Fordingbridge. There are also one or two small streams which rise in the New Forest and join the main river between Ringwood and Winkton, the largest of these being the Ripley Brook. None of these streams is of great consequence. The Allen in its upper reaches is a chalk fed winter bourne, rising near Martin village close to the Salisbury-Blandford turnpike road. It is big enough to hold trout in its lower reaches; while the Ripley brook running in near Sopley from the New Forest peat lands has an acid content, and largely for that reason provides spawning grounds for sea-trout, which have a marked preference for such water. The other streams from the New Forest are fed by sources in its sand and gravel. These small tributaries have little effect on the main river, except after a heavy downpour when for a short time their combined flow is considerable.

From Pewsey to Christchurch the Avon falls a total of 354 feet, giving it an average fall of approximately 5 feet per mile, this fall being steepest upstream of Salisbury.

At Christchurch, there is the well known Knapp Mill, belonging to the West Hampshire Water company, the fishing here being known as the 'Royalty'. This fishery has been renowned over the past 150 years or even longer, both for its salmon and coarse fish (of which more later). The Dorset Stour joins the Avon in its tidal reaches below the Royalty fishery and close to its mouth.

Christchurch itself has a long and interesting history. After Salisbury it is the most famous of the Avon's towns, so a few words about its story may not come amiss.

An abbey and a castle were built here shortly after the Norman

Invasion of 1066. The former lasted until the Dissolution of the Monasteries under King Henry VIII, and the latter until the 17th century Civil War, when it was demolished. The magnificent Priory, still in full commission at this present time, was built in 1100 AD by Ralf (or Rolf) Flambard, then Bishop of Durham, but was added to and completed under King Henry VII in 1509. Its tower stands erect in a fine setting on high ground, close above the junction of Avon and Stour, and is visible from many miles distant. Perhaps the best view of it is from Hengistbury Head on its south side.

This Priory contains a number of interesting monuments, and its choir stalls are said to be older than those of Westminster Abbey. A notable legend is attached to the story of its construction, which runs as follows. It was intended in the first place to build the Priory on the nearby St. Catherine's Hill, but each night after building was begun there materials were mysteriously removed to the present site. The workers took this to be a sign of divine intervention, and started to build the Priory where it now stands. During the course of construction a carpenter appeared and assisted in the work, but would accept no remuneration. He finally vanished without trace, giving rise to the belief that he was Christ Himself, and the Priory, and subsequently the town, were named accordingly.

Christchurch was undoubtedly a port of considerable significance in Anglo-Saxon and early mediaeval times, until ships became too large to enter its harbour, when it yielded place to Southampton and Poole. By degrees the combined silt brought down by the Avon and Stour, or washed in from the sea, formed a barrier to the open sea at Mudeford, in the form of a huge sandbank. The river water kept a passage open through this sandbank in a comparatively narrow channel known as the 'Run', while inshore from this outlet was formed a wide expanse of water like an inland tidal lake, known as Christchurch Harbour. During the reign of King Charles II work was actually started in an attempt to recreate a great harbour here, and a pier and a wharf were built. But all this work eventually came to nothing. Now this 'Harbour' is the delight of holiday makers and boating parties. It has long been lost to any form of commerce.

A stretch on the Royalty water. Edwards Pool and Hayters Pool left and right of island

Between Ringwood and Christchurch the valley has changed in character. It is wider, to correspond with the Avon's increased flow, and no longer does the river flow through a chalk countryside, dividing Wiltshire's downlands. By now it is bordering instead the heathlands typical of the New Forest. In this area it flows over a bed of clay and tertiary sands, though still interspersed widely with silt and less frequently with gravel. Extensive water meadows still border its course; but on either side, if investigation is made away back from the river, a heath country will be found, often thickly wooded, with an acid soil which in May and June produces an abundant crop of rhododendrons. As elsewhere, the haycrop in the water meadows is luxuriant; and the lovely summer weather ushered in by the cuckoo's first call in late April provides in them a never ending source of delight. Whether fishing or merely passing by, one is surrounded by so many fascinating forms of wildlife of every sort. There is always something of interest to watch, or to listen to, or to examine. As river keeper Frank Sawyer of Netheravon expressed it: 'Each season of the year has it attractions; as the weeks change to months, so change the character and appearance of the river, and the life of the river and riverside creatures. The angler need never be lonely, for he learns to understand and appreciate the wildlife which are his constant companions.'

It could not be put more concisely; but of all the months in the year it would surely be generally agreed that May and June take the garland, with April and July following close in their steps.

During the winter months, needless to say, water meadows such as the Avon's become bleaker, windier and colder, and their vegetation dies down. Occasionally the river overflows its banks and floods all around, to the delight of gulls and waterfowl of all sorts. White front and Canada geese appear in numbers, as do Bewick's swans, duck of many sorts, and snipe. There are some excellent water meadow shoots. The best are at Somerley, Bisterne, and Avon Tyrrell, but there are other good ones further upstream, as well as on the Frome and on other rivers elsewhere in the neighbourhood. Coot and moorhen are considerably decreased on the lower Avon however because the mink prey upon them.

AVON FISHING

Salmon

The history of salmon fishing in the Hampshire Avon goes back a long way. Net fishing by far predated rod fishing, and was certainly being systematically carried out by 1814, when Grimble, in his *Salmon Rivers of England and Wales* (1904), recorded the net catch for that year at Knapp Mill (the Royalty Fishing) as being of 1600 fish. This is more than twice as many as the average net catch at Mudeford on the mouth of the Avon in present times, and no doubt net fishing even by then had long been practised.

By 1862, however, Grimble points out that intensive netting had nearly exterminated Avon salmon. A fixed hang-net had for many years been worked all round the clock immediately outside of Christchurch Harbour, and there was another such net of around 200 yards length often fished within the Harbour.

These two nets had a total catch of only one hundred and ninety fish during the three years 1860, 1861 and 1862. At Knapp Mill, situated close to the high tide mark in the Avon about half a mile upstream of Christchurch, there was also what was known as a 'fishing dam.' A net was worked immediately below it, and its catch in 1860, 1861 and 1862 was only sixty eight, fifty eight and seventy three salmon respectively. A mile or so above this was a further 'fishing dam' at Winkton, where another net was worked. These two dams between them went far to prevent the upstream passage of anything but a small remnant of fish.

Here was a classic example of the stock of salmon, in what should have been a prolific river, being pared down by ruthless and indiscriminate commercial fishing to a fraction of its proper yield. The above figures illustrate only too clearly the decrease of Avon salmon stocks during the period 1814–1862.

In this latter year, however, things were taken in hand. The fixed nets at the mouth of the river and in the harbour were declared illegal, and fish passes were constructed at the Knapp Mill weir and at the Winkton weir, which made the passage of fish easier. There were many more breeding fish in the river as a result. In addition, shortly after this, a Fishery Board was formed and passes were made in the weirs at Ringwood and above. This was a great step forward; though some of these passes, notably the one at Ringwood itself, proved inefficient.

From now on the take of the nets at the 'Run', the narrow outlet at Mudeford from Christchurch Harbour into the open sea, steadily improved. By 1869 the return of catch here was 652 fish, compared to 40 in 1860. The Royalty net also continued to fish at this time, and it can be assumed that its catch, although not declared, improved correspondingly with that of the 'Run'.

From 1869 until 1881, the net catch (exclusive of the Royalty's) averaged 646 fish per year (varying between 1060 highest, and 358 lowest). Rod fishing also began to be taken up more seriously during these years and averaged 34 fish per year, (also exclusive of the Royalty's catch). As a matter of interest in this connection it was recorded that a salmon of 12 lb was caught by rod on trout tackle at Bisterne by Sir Charles Smedley as early as April 1770. It is not thought likely however that rod fishing was much practised before the latter half of the Victorian era.

The biggest two fish caught up to date by 1881 were $48\frac{1}{2}$ lb by rod and 47 lb by net, and the average size was around 20 lb.

Between 1882 and 1902 the net catch averaged 819, and the rod catch 105. The average weight again was around 20 lb. So both nets and rods appear to have done better during this period, but it must always be remembered that the above figures are not complete, since the Royalty catch by both nets and rods up to then was never declared. Rod fishing in those days also would have been far less intensive than now, by far fewer rods, perhaps only four or five per day at the most on the whole river. Little or no salmon fishing was done upstream of Ringwood.

Here are further total net and rod catch yearly averages of salmon

and grilse over ten year periods up to 1972 and shorter periods thereafter: these figures include the Royalty rod catch, at any rate from
1921 onwards.

Date	Nets (yearly average)	Rods (yearly average)
1903–1912	449	63
1913–1922	805	154
1923–1932	261	152
1933–1942	527	240
1943–1952	287	215
1953–1962	668	639
1963–1972	1047	580
1973–1975	702	540
1976–1978	531	255
1979–1981	728	582
1982	531	428
1983	650	668
1984	867	768
1985	503	656

The highest catches by rod were in 1955 and 1956, when 1196
fish and 977 fish were caught.

It will be seen that the most prolific returns were between 1953
and 1975, and that since that time catches have declined to some
extent, though not markedly so.

What has changed in a notable manner, however, is the size and
type of fish entering the river over recent years. Up to about 1955
the Avon salmon were almost exclusively big spring fish of three
or even four sea-winters. Their average weight was high, at least
19 lb, and in some years it rose to 23 lb. Thirty pounders were common, and one or two forty pounders were caught on one beat or
another during most seasons. The record rod-caught fish weighed
$49\frac{1}{2}$ lb. It was taken on February 27th, 1952, by Mr. G. M. Howard,
in the Green Banks pool above the railway bridge on the Royalty
water, on a silver sprat. Mr. Howard also caught two other fish of
$41\frac{1}{2}$ lb and 41 lb on the Royalty both in 1951. At least eleven fish
of over 40 lb have been landed at Avon Tyrrell during this century,

the biggest being 48 lb. Bisterne, too, produced a 48 pounder to Mrs. Shawe's rod in April, 1936; and another of $48\frac{1}{2}$ lb was taken near Ringwood by Mr. Gladstone that same year. In fact, forty pounders were not rare in those days, and most beats as far upstream as Somerley had their quota of them. It is doubtful whether any other river in Britain has at any time yielded fish of higher average weight; though of course many of them produced much more numerous catches and many fish of higher individual weights. It is curious, for instance, that the Avon in spite of its many 40 pounders has never yielded a 50 pounder, while other 'big fish' rivers such as the Tay, Tweed, Wye and Awe have produced them in numbers.

Mrs. Shawe with her record Bisterne salmon, 48 lb. 1936

Up to the mid-1950's two sea-winter fish of 10 lb to 14 lb were comparatively scarce in the Avon, and grilse almost unknown. But from that time onwards a change has set in. The big spring fish have gradually become ever scarcer, and the smaller 10 to 14 pounders have much increased. These latter now form the principal salmon stock, while the bigger class of spring fish has dwindled. In addition to this, an extensive grilse run, from late June onwards, now takes place. This run has markedly increased over the past fifteen or so years, and now forms a substantial part of the catch. Although occasional big spring fish are still taken, for instance in 1984 Mr. A. Cherry had one of 38 lb (on fly) at Avon Tyrrell and another of the same weight was caught in 1985 at Bisterne, as a whole this change both in weight and type of fish is most striking and is greatly regretted by the older generation of Avon anglers. The average weight of rod-caught Avon fish is now down to 11 lb.

An interesting speculation in connection with the decrease of large spring fish and the build-up of smaller salmon and grilse concerns the point that the springers are considerably more vulnerable to rod fishing than the two latter classes of smaller fish. They enter the river earlier, when fishing conditions are better, i.e. when the water temperature is at a good level, with the river at a good fishing height, and with the weed not thickly grown. They are also at risk from rod fishing over an appreciably longer period of the season than summer salmon or grilse. It might be estimated therefore that a considerably higher proportion of these fish would be likely to be caught by rod than of the later running fish which enter the river under less good fishing conditions nearer the end of the season. This may partly account for their present scarcity, particularly as the number of rods normally on the river in present times has at least doubled since 1954 and about trebled since 1939.

What is more, there has in the year 1953 been an investigation by Dr. Margaret Brown into the number of fish which enter the Avon as second time spawners, having already spawned in a previous year. Of thirty-seven hen fish then examined, seven were found to be second spawners. This indicated that as much as 20% of the spawning stock were likely to be second spawners. Dr. Margaret pointed out the disastrous cumulative effect on both overall and spawning stocks if anything went seriously wrong with the return of fish of this type, and one is inclined to wonder in these present times how far such a latent threat has materialized.

Another factor about present-day Avon salmon which should be noticed is the increased extent of their river habitat. Mention has already been made above of the limiting factor to the run in Victorian times in the shape of the weirs at the Royalty and Winkton, close to the mouth. By degrees, obstacles such as these were made passable, and above Winkton there is no set of hatches until Ringwood. For many years fish were held up by these latter, until in the early 1930's, largely at the instigation of Sir John Mills of Bisterne (see page 81), an improved ladder was built there. At once the fishing upstream, particularly at Somerley, was improved, whereas before this all worthwhile salmon fishing had rightly been considered to end at Ringwood. In the 1960's, when the Ringwood road by-pass was built, an entirely new set of hatches and a new and efficient ladder was constructed at Ringwood. Now there is no obstruction whatever to the passage of fish at this point.

Above Ringwood there are hatches at Ibsley, which are kept wide open and present no obstacle to fish. Further upstream there are a series of hatches, the main ones being at Bickton, Breamore, Downton, Standlynch, and Britford. Some of these undoubtedly check fish in their upstream passage, but the Wessex Water Authority plans to put in ladders wherever they may be necessary. This should be of substantial help to the salmon, and over the years may lead to considerable increase in stock, as well as to improvement in fishing in the upper river.

At the moment the main salmon spawning area in the Avon lies between Downton and Salisbury in the main river, and also for a further short distance up tributaries such as the Nadder and Wylye, and to a lesser extent the Ebble and Bourne. There is good spawning ground further upstream in all of these rivers, and if the salmon were encouraged to penetrate further there is little doubt that this again,

PLATE 4

A view of the Avon at Somerley

Avon Hatches at Ringwood and salmon ladder

PLATE 5

Snow at Ibsley, painted by Paul Stewart

in due course, would lead to an eventual increase in stock. General observation and experience goes to show that, other things being equal, the wider the distribution of good spawning ground in a river the greater the stock of salmon and grilse which a river can carry. So the future prospects for Avon salmon stocks seem promising. On the other hand, presence of spawning salmon in the good trout waters higher upstream might not always be welcome. This is a recurring problem in south country rivers, not only here but in the Test and Itchen as well. Forbearance and goodwill should provide a solution. In any case, since chalk stream trout fishing nowadays is so largely dependent on stocking and so little on the wild trout, it would not seem that the presence of a limited number of spawning salmon and their progeny would do much harm; and incidentally the adult trout in the upper river would have a fine meal of salmon ova and salmon fry.

An interesting fact, confirmed by J. W. Jones, D.Sc., Ph.D., in his book *The Salmon* (1959), is that 90 per cent of Avon salmon smolts are yearlings. This quick growth is obviously due to the excellent chalk stream food supply for fry and parr. What effect it may have on the timing of their subsequent return from the sea as adult fish is uncertain. Two completely contrary theoretical results of this quick growth have been suggested in the past. One is that it produces an adult return mainly of one sea-winter grilse, the other that it produces big three or four sea-winter fish such as the Avon springers of former times. Neither theory is totally convincing; and they are in complete contradiction to each other, particularly in view of the recent change from the preponderance of big springers to that of small salmon and grilse. What is certain, however, is that Avon smolts compare favourably in size and growth rate to those of most other British rivers, where smolts are normally two and often three years old.

The net catch at Mudeford at the mouth of the Avon is considerable. Recent declared catches have been already quoted (see p. 61).

The figures go to show that the net catch has remained fairly constant over the past twenty years, though the average size of fish caught, as in the case of the rod catch, has declined. The bulk of the net catch is now made from the second half of June until the end of July when the water is low, a large proportion of fish then caught being grilse.

As already pointed out, net fishing on the Avon in the main predated rod fishing by a long period of time. Grimble gives the Avon rod catch for the 1896 season as 10 fish. It is unlikely that rod fishing went back to any great extent before that year, while by 1814 we know that netting was in full swing. There is still a public right of netting in the 'Run' at Mudeford , though the Water Authority has the power to limit the number of net licences. At present this number is seven. The existence of this public right, however, would make the purchase of the netting rights a very intricate if not impossible business, should any person or group of persons ever contemplate it.

The legal net fishing season for salmon in the Avon lasts from February 1st to July 31st each year, and for sea-trout from April 15th to July 31st. The weekly close time is from 6 am on Saturdays to 6 am on Mondays, also between 9 pm on each of the evenings of Wednesday, Thursday, and Friday every week until 6 am on the respective following mornings. (This was a new form of 'slap', introduced on the Avon comparatively recently. It is believed that it has more lately been adopted or is at least under consideration elsewhere.) In fact, however, little netting is done at Mudeford before April each year.

The method of net fishing at Mudeford is comparatively simple, and a brief description of it is as follows. This fishing is always carried out from the right-hand bank of the 'Run' i.e. the narrow outlet from the wide expanse of Christchurch Harbour into the open sea. This outlet is some 200 yards long by 50/60 yards wide, and the tide both ebbs and flows through it.

The seine net of the type used is not allowed to be of more than 185 metres in length or 7.5 metres in depth. One end of the net is held fast onto the shore, while the rest is paid out from a row-boat, which is propelled not more than three quarters of the way across the channel and then on downstream, with the net being paid out

Salmon netting in the 'Run' at Mudeford. See also Plate 7, page 97

all the time. When the full length of the net has been shot, the boat is pulled back to the right bank with the downstream end of the net towed after it. The net is then hauled ashore, with any catch it may have made.

It will be realized that a method such as this can only be used on the ebb tide, or else at the very start of the flood tide when there is still a downstream current in the top part of the 'Run'. This is when the fish come in. A crew of three men makes the operation easier, though it is possible with only two, one in the boat and one on the bank.

Only one net is allowed to be in operation at any one time; so the seven licensees, or as many of them as are present, have to take it in turn to shoot their net. Twenty to thirty shots of the net can usually be made on one ebb tide, and the 'Run' at Mudeford is the only netting station, though occasional shots of the net are also made slightly higher upstream at the bottom end of Christchurch Harbour.

It can be seen from this short account of both method and close times that the netting of salmon and sea-trout is by no means excessive at Mudeford compared to that at many other netting stations on other British rivers.

Turning to the subject of pollution, this in the past has been a cause of serious concern in the Avon. It was bad in the Salisbury area, until the construction of the modern sewage works at Petersfinger in the 1950's. There was also serious pollution in the past at Christchurch. But both these sources of impurity have now been efficiently dealt with, and the water of the Avon runs satisfactorily pure from source to mouth.

A new cause of anxiety is the presence of a large number of fish farms on the Avon and its tributaries. There are at present no less than twenty seven of these, rearing for the most part either brown or rainbow trout. There is no limit to the amount of water which each of these farms can legally divert from the river to flow through its stews and back to the river again. Some of the fish farms are very large, and the total number of trout they contain must run into millions. Although no harm is done if the outlet streams from these farms remain pure, there is an obvious danger of disease occurring amongst such large artificial concentrations of fish. Such disease could well spread into the river amongst wild fish, which would be a calamity. There is also a danger of smolts on their downstream migration being trapped against the stew inlet screens and killed. So the whole position is an uneasy one; and, particularly if fish farms increase in number, no one can forecast with certainty whether or not their long-term effect will produce any change in the balance of wild fish population, whether of salmon, trout or coarse fish.

FISHING THE RIVER

To return to rod fishing for salmon, and all that goes with it, the Avon is spring-fed, as already pointed out; its water is fairly clear in that part of the river which lies downstream of Salisbury (i.e. where nearly all the salmon fishing takes place), but not so clear as it used to be in times gone past. For some reason nowadays there is usually a certain cloudiness in it, the cause of which is difficult to pin-point, though possibly it results from improved general drainage. The basic cause of this cloudiness, reduced to scientific terms, is the presence of diatoms or microscopic algae, which thrive in cold water and bright sun. These appear to be a comparatively new phenomenon in the Avon, though long known in the Stour. In any case this impurity is not sufficient to do any harm to the fishing. Only after exceptionally heavy rain does this river colour to any extent. Nor is it affected by sudden rises or falls, such as occur in hill-country streams. The catchment area is comparatively flat and the bulk of the rainfall does not run off as surface water, but sinks into the chalk subsoil to emerge later from springs, and so flow into the river or its tributaries. The heaviest rainfall is during late autumn and winter, and the underground water table is apt to rise until about February. It is during January, February and March that the springs, provided they are not affected by hard frost, put forth their biggest outflow. After a normal or heavy winter's rainfall they maintain a good flow in the Avon at least until June, and even after that the river only falls moderately. This type of heavy flow is of great advantage for fishing, as it enables salmon to run upriver whenever they feel so inclined, and without waiting for a rise in water level. It also keeps the water in good fishing order for most of the time.

It is true that the Avon has a deep slow and solid flow, running in high water at an average of about 4 knots, and in low water at half that speed or less. It has no obvious pools such as occur in a north country river, and few shallows. In fact, it looks altogether very unlikely as a salmon river to those who do not know it; and anglers whose previous experience has been confined to the north country might well refuse at first sight to believe that it is one at all.

The fish are inclined to prefer deep holes or deep pools. They do not like the shallows, but are usually found in water of four feet or more in depth, either at the neck or the tail of the deeps. It is difficult for someone who does not know the river to judge where the lies are likely to be. A pronounced bend is apt to provide a lie, and where the current is steady flowing, rather than boiling. On the other hand, boils on the surface indicate weed clumps or outcrops of some sort on the bottom, and fish sometimes like to lie upstream of these, or to one side of them. And where there are hatches fish usually pause, either above them, or downstream in the tail of the main rush, or in the backflow on either side under the bank.

On the whole, lies do not change much and are liable to remain in the same area year after year. After big winter floods, however, new lies can form, when the contours of the river-bed have changed, or when banks have fallen in or crumbled; and occasionally a well-established lie for no apparent reason will cease to hold fish for a year or two. Changes in the pattern of weed growth are another factor which can affect lies. Salmon usually enjoy the shelter which clumps of good weed, such as ranunculus, give them. Not that they bury themselves in it, but they like to lie in the clear gravel patches or channels between the weed growth and prefer a stretch of river with a fair amount of weed to one that, for one reason or another, is bare of it. Weed also gives fish shade from bright summer sun, and in daylight helps to oxygenate the water. As well as this it also helps to accelerate the flow when this latter is confined to channels between weed clumps, and so to keep a gravel patch clear which may well provide a lie. It does therefore have its advantages.

Another way in which lies can be recognized is if fish more than once jump in the same place. If they constantly show in any likely looking place, it is an obvious indication of a lie, as can easily be realized. But actually this is not such a helpful indication as it sounds, because it must be admitted that fish seldom show in the Avon, and one never finds a pool full of jumping fish, as for instance on some well-stocked Highland river. In actual fact, it is rare to see an Avon fish jump at all; and if one is seen it is worth fishing over where it showed, even if this looks an unlikely place. The fish in question *may* be a runner, but on the other hand it may not; and if not it will quite probably take.

To sum up on this question of finding lies, the whole process to a new incomer is a difficult one, and experience is by far the best teacher. Of course, on the other hand, if one can find some local expert who is kind enough to walk the river with one in the first place and point out all the likely places, this is of the greatest value. Such advice should never be scorned, and should be meticulously memorized. It may save many hours of fruitless experiment.

The Avon rod fishing season lasts from February 1st to September 30th. The early spring, during February and March, now produces few fish, except at the bottom beat, the Royalty. There is, however, still the chance of an odd big fish at this time of year, as there is also in April, which is generally a better month. May and June are the most prolific months although with smaller fish; July too is now-adays improving, though the water is sometimes apt to get too warm and too weedy. August and September are of no great value, though coarse fishermen then catch a certain number of grilse.

It goes without saying that on the Avon as elsewhere it pays the angler to have the best quality tackle which he can possibly obtain. It is a bad mistake ever to be content with less. Indifferent tackle always lets its owner down in due course; and even if the best is more expensive, it works out cheaper in the end, as it lasts far longer.

Avon fish in the spring still run large, averaging around 16/17 lb. Nylon monofilament of a minimum of 15 lb breaking strain is needed, and 20 lb is often better. In summer it is unwise to use less than 10 lb breaking strain, and 12 lb is none too light. There is nothing more infuriating than to be broken by a good fish through the use of too fine a cast or trace.

Now some words on the process of fishing. Undoubtedly, Avon salmon are more easily caught on bait, rather than on fly. The causes of this are many. Usually the stream is too slow for a fly to fish attractively, also the fish are apt to lie too deep for them to rise readily to a fly near the surface. A bait, on the other hand, can be fished slowly and almost down to their mouths. A further and perhaps more pertinent disadvantage for fly fishing is that salmon often lie close under an almost perpendicular bank. Thus the fly, from whichever side it is fished, cannot swing over them (which is such an effective tactic in the open pools of a north country river). If fished from the deep side over such fish, it can only hang or be drawn upstream, which is probably not attractive enough, or if fished from the shallow side such fish probably do not notice it at all. A bait on the other hand, at least if fished from the deep side, can be brought attractively to within inches of the fish's mouth and, if necessary, held there. Only if the fish is lying some little distance from either bank can a fly be made to fish over it in a really enticing manner. So a fair proportion of the lies do not lend themselves to fly fishing with any real prospect of success.

Floating cut weed is also another hazard to fly fishing, as it is to bait fishing but more so. Weed has to be cut at periods in order to avoid flooding, and a certain amount of cut weed is always liable to appear in the lower Avon, in endless bits and pieces. If frequent enough, such shreds of weed can cause the angler constant annoyance by fouling his line or lure. Apart from at recognized weed-cutting times, they can be particularly troublesome if the water rises to any extent after rain. It is much easier, however, for the bait fisherman to manoeuvre his line so as to dodge such pieces of weed. A fly fisherman, with his line and fly fishing near the surface can find this almost impossible; and he can be driven off the river if the cut weed becomes too thick. (It helps however to avoid the floating weed if he fishes with a sunk line.)

All these factors combined make it difficult to catch fish on a fly, and a bait fisherman almost always has a better chance of success. The result is that bait fishermen on this river by far outnumber fly fishermen, and it is safe to say that eleven out of every twelve Avon fish are caught on bait of one sort or another. Baits most frequently used are wooden devon minnows and Toby or Mepps spoons, while prawns, shrimps, plugs and worms, though banned until May 15th, after that date are used extensively. In the view of some Avon fishermen and fishery owners it would be good move if prawn, shrimp and worm were totally banned in the interests of conservation of stock; but full agreement over such measures seems unlikely at present to be achieved.

Mrs. Fearfield fishing at Somerley

Fishing in the Avon is all from the bank; there is virtually no wading, except on occasions at knee depth on a sandbank. Gumboots or, at the most, thigh waders are all that is needed. A gaff should always be carried. It is the only effective instrument for landing a big fish when the angler is by himself. A landing net of a light portable type is alright for small fish or grilse, but is of little use for anything of much over 20 lb. Tailers are on the whole inefficient and certainly far less practical than a long shafted gaff, and beaching is seldom possible, as the banks almost without exception are too high above the water level. A priest is another piece of equipment

that every angler should carry. Once a fish has been landed a couple
of quick blows with this between the eyes are a quick and merciful
way to adminster the *coup de grâce*. This seems to be his fair due
after the magnificent sport he will certainly have given, and stones or
other makeshift implements are rarely to be found in water meadows.

One other item which should certainly be included in the kit is
a good pair of polaroid glasses. These are a great help. Not only do
they sometimes make it possible in time of low water to spot a fish
lying on the bottom, but at all times they act as useful sun-glasses
and save the eyes from glare. They also act as a windshield if the
breeze is strong, and as a protection to the eyes from the stray hooks
of mistimed casts. Apart from this polaroid glasses in every way help
visibility both above and below water level, and are a great boon.

The actual process of fishing is much the same on the Avon as
on other salmon rivers, with one important exception. It pays on
this river, as on the Frome, and Test, to fish very slowly, i.e. not
to hurry in fishing out the cast, and often to let the bait hang for
some moments in a likely lie. Even more important is to take only
a short step in a downstream direction between successive casts. One
has often heard the theory that 'it is better to fish a pool down twice
quickly than once slowly'. This may well be true on north country
rivers, with their big stocks of fish and large, well-defined pools;
but it is certainly not true on south country rivers such as the Avon,
Frome, and Test. On these, one can hardly fish too deliberately, and
one needs to proceed very slowly and very carefully, yard by yard,
and almost foot by foot. In addition, one needs great accuracy in
casting when the fish are lying close to the opposite bank. The fly
or bait has to drop not within feet but within *inches* of the far side
if it is to stand any chance of attracting such fish. This again is a
factor of the greatest importance.

If you rise or pull a fish, and he does not take hold, give him a
minute or so before you try him again. In the meantime make a heel
mark at the exact spot where you are standing, to be sure of finding
it again later if so wanted. The point of the pause is to give the fish
time to return to his lie, should he have moved out of it. Some people,

Colonel Kidston-Montgomerie fishing at Somerley

particularly ladies, find it impossible to restrain themselves in these circumstances from immediately casting again! and if you fall into such a category there is a simple answer—shorten your line by two or three yards, and standing in the same place start casting again, gradually lengthening the line between casts, until you are finally throwing exactly the same length as before. Thus you effect the desired pause before covering the fish once more. If at the second time of covering him he rises or pulls again, it is worth keeping at him at intervals until he finally takes hold or loses interest; but never be in too much of a hurry over this. It is often worth while returning to him after an hour or so elsewhere, or even finally at the end of the day. Somewhere it has been written or said: 'Softly, softly, catchee monkey!'. This advice is applicable to a fishing situation of this sort.

Playing hooked fish in the Avon is comparatively simple. They seldom have room to run out a long line, and with the heavy tackle used in spring it is a rather brutal business. Only trees or bushes along the bank, or occasionally side streams, hatches, or bridges, form the rare obstructions past which the angler cannot follow his fish. Also there is never a really strong current to help the hooked fish. The result is that landing a thirty pounder in the Avon with all due respect to such a fish is often a simpler and quicker task than landing a sixteen or twenty pounder in a river like the Spey or Dee. From May onwards growing clumps of weed, however, can form tiresome obstructions when a fish is hooked. Unlike trout, hooked salmon do not deliberately immerse themselves in weed and hang on to it. But if they run out any length of line, and turn and twist to any extent, it is quite likely that, by accident as it were, they will get the line entangled in weed growth. They usually come free after a short interval; but if they don't the angler's best plan is to get downstream of where the line enters the weed and handline, gently to start with, but with gradually increasing pressure. This almost always achieves the desired result, even if it takes a little time; and it should be rare to lose a fish through weed entanglement (though occasionally, of course, it inevitably happens).

Other obstructions on the bed of the river are scarce. There are no boulders, or sharp rocks, or anything worse than an occasional sunken bough which should in any case have been previously removed. So playing a fish, even on the lighter tackle used in summer, should present no great difficulty. Only if a very large fish of, say, 35 lb or over is hooked, and the angler has no one with him to help him land it, should any really uphill struggle have to be faced.

As mentioned above, it is difficult to catch fish on a fly in the Avon, but by no means impossible. It was only recently in 1984 (see p. 63) that a 38 pounder was caught on fly at Avon Tyrrell, and landed in twenty minutes; a fine performance. May and June, when the water becomes lower and warmer, and when fish are more numerous, are the best fly months. In early spring, up to mid April, if the angler prefers to use fly, he needs heavy tackle. A carbon rod of sixteen feet is neither too long nor too heavy, and a slow sinking line or at least a floating line with a sinking tip is wanted. A big tube fly with a brass body and hair wing is the best lure, mounted on a sizeable treble hook and fished on monofilament of at least 15 lb breaking strain. A rod of such a length is desirable, partly because the wind at this time of year can be troublesome and partly because it gives better control of line and fly as they are fished round. With carbon graphite as a rod material, there is now no objection to a rod of this length on the ground of weight.

Later in the season, with the approach of summer, a rod of 14 feet or even 13 feet will be found adequate, though there is still no harm in using a longer rod if this is preferred. Flies can be reduced in size, tied on treble or double hooks, which take a better hold than single hooks; but there is never any need to drop to the very small sizes of fly which one sometimes sees used elsewhere. Size 6 is the smallest one need occasionally descend to. Monofilament should be of 10 or 12 lb breaking strain, not less and fished with a floating line. A good pattern of fly reel is desirable, big enough to hold dressed line and 100 yards of 20 lb backing. Cheap fly reels are a mistake. They usually go wrong in one way or another fairly soon, while a first class reel as already mentioned will last a lifetime.

Accuracy in casting is essential, particularly when fish are lying close to the far bank. A good fisherman should possess the ability to land his fly within an inch or two of the far bank, even in the face of a strong adverse wind. It is not always easy.

When fishing a floating line, the angler should invariably be on the watch for a V or a boil in the water, indicating that a fish has moved at his fly without touching it. This is of the greatest import- ance, and as summer advances more and more fish are liable to adopt this procedure. They go through the motions of rising, so to speak, without actually touching the fly. It is an infuriating habit, but fre- quently occurs. Such fish can sometimes be induced to take after a suitable interval, or if fished faster or in a different way. That is why it is so important to watch for the original rise, and carefully to mark the exact spot where one is standing when it occurs, so as to be sure of returning later to the right place if one has left it for the time being.

If one sees a fish jump or head and tail, one should at once go and fish over him. Fish in the Avon, as noted above, rarely show; (but when they do they are often takers.) On a good fishing day, for example, several fish may be caught without a single one having been seen to show. It is difficult to detect exactly the reason for this; but possibly it is because fish are more likely to show when congregated in numbers, and when one or two restless fish will disturb others; while lying more isolated, as in the Avon, they are likelier to remain quiet. (As a matter of interest it is said that in the old days, when spring fish were much more numerous, these fish used to show a good deal more than the present day fish.)

When a fish takes he should be held firmly at the start, to make sure that the hook's points have penetrated beyond the barb. If held too lightly, and the barbs have not got a hold, he may easily get rid of the hooks by shaking his head or jumping. This naturally applies anywhere, and not only on the Avon.

The process of playing a fish has already been described, and it is similar with a fly as it is with a bait, except that it may take slightly longer. It is also rather more difficult with the longer fly rod to bring the fish within easy reach of the gaff or net if one is by oneself. Don't become impatient in this case, but just take things easily. It should all come right in the end if one is prepared to keep calm and wait till the fish is played out. Don't have wild shots with the gaff while the fish is still lively, or still deep in the water. More often than not this leads to trouble. At all times try to keep opposite or slightly downstream of your fish, and if he runs fast upstream or downstream, move as quickly as possible, without stumbling, to get opposite again.

One final word, as to water temperature. The angler, whether or not he is actually carrying a thermometer at the time, should make it his business to be aware of the temperature within a degree or two. Cold water of, say, 43°F or less means large flies and baits; but as it gets warmer the size should lessen, until when it reaches the 60°s F all lures should be fairly small. For fly fishing a floating line becomes desirable when the temperature reaches around 52°F or above. To a large extent, therefore, the water temperature provides a ready-reckoner for the choice of fly or bait; but when the air is markedly colder than the water fish take badly and need a lure well sunk.

BEATS ON THE RIVER

The main beats on the Avon, working upstream from Christchurch, are as follows:—

The Royalty Fishery. This lies at the tidal part of the river, over a distance of about three quarters of a mile. It has two principal hatches, one on the main river at the Great Weir, and one at what is known as 'The Parlour' at Knapp Mill on a separate branch of the river. There are salmon ladders in both. Four rods are allowed on this beat at a time. The fishery is owned by the West Hampshire Water Company. (Further information about the Royalty is given on pages 88–93 below.)

Winkton. This beat lies next above the Royalty. It has two hatches, but these are kept wide open at all times and are no obstacle to the passage of fish. The owner of this fishing is Major John Mills, of Bisterne. Its length is about 2 miles.

Avon Tyrrell. This fishing extends for around 2 miles upstream of Winkton, and is owned by Lord Manners. It is divided into two beats, each for two rods.

Bisterne. A longer fishery of some 3 miles in length, upstream of Avon Tyrrell and about $2\frac{1}{2}$ miles below Ringwood. This fishery also belongs to Major John Mills. It is divided into three beats, with a maximum of two rods on each beat. For further details of Bisterne see pages 81-87.

The Several Fishery. This fishery extends from Ringwood for two and a half miles downstream to march with Bisterne. It belongs to Mr. R. Ferguson.

Somerley. This is the longest fishery on this part of the river. It belongs to the Earl of Normanton, and extends for about $3\frac{1}{2}$ miles from just above Ibsley down to Ringwood. There are six beats on it for two rods apiece. Somerley is a well known fishery, visited by anglers from far and wide. In a good season it produces a fair number of fish, perhaps 150 or more, though in a bad one as few as 20 or 30. Of late years its catch has been on the whole disappointing, and it seems that nowadays fish tend to run through it more quickly than in the past. It is however an agreeable stretch of water amid very pleasant surroundings. There are two hatch pools on it below Ibsley Bridge, near to its upper boundary, which add to its attractions. It also has fishing on the left bank of the Ringwood hatch pool.

N.B. All the above fisheries have both banks for almost all their length.

There are one or two other short pieces of water, separately owned, but of no great extent.

Above Somerley there are a number of fishings, privately owned, for as far upstream as Wilton on the Nadder and Wylye, above Salisbury. The longest of these at Longford belongs to Lord Radnor. But the best of the fishing lies downstream of Fordingbridge, and it is only in a high water year that fish run much further upriver before the spawning season. In such a year the Longford fishing is the best in this area.

Which is normally the best beat of all? This query is often made, and undoubtedly the answer is the Royalty, which produces more fish early in the season than any other beat, and continues to provide good fishing right into the summer. The next best fishing is probably at Somerley, though part of its best beat unfortunately has been sold not long ago. Bickton, above Somerley, also produces a fair quantity of fish, though most of them at present are caught in one small hatch pool. Upstream of this the catch is doubtful; and it is usually only a question of the odd fish, though Longford has produced as many as sixty in a high water season.

Bisterne

No account of Avon salmon fishing would be complete without reference to the late Sir John Mills of Bisterne, who achieved more than any other individual, before or since, for its benefit. Sir John lived from 1879 to 1972, and spent most of his life on his estate at Bisterne near Ringwood. He was a most kindly and considerate person, small of stature yet spry and upright even into his nineties, and of outstanding general ability. He was also a great all-round sportsman, a dedicated salmon fisherman, and an exceptional game shot. The Bisterne sporting records coupled with his own personal fishing journal show that between 1903 and 1965 (although he did little fishing after 1942) he accounted for no less than 310 salmon on the Avon at Bisterne and Winkton, of the remarkable average weight of $21\frac{1}{2}$ lb. Few if any fishermen on the Avon can have approached such a score. It was not only the numbers that were outstanding but even more so the high average weight of these fish. Two of his fish were of 40 lb, and three of 38 lb. In addition he caught 25 other fish of 30 lb or over, and 39 of his above fish were taken on a fly.

Apart from the Avon, Sir John fished other rivers, for instance the Dee, Conon, Carron, Deveron, Wye and Test. On these he caught a further total of 31 fish, mostly on fly.

One particular salmon that he lost, as happens in the case of many fishermen, was perhaps the biggest he ever hooked. The story as recounted by Mr. J. C. S. Mills, Sir John's youngest son, runs as follows:

'My father told me that one evening he was fishing the Lower Osier Bed from the west bank and, just as he was about to go home for dinner, he saw a very big fish jump right at the tail of the pool. He could stay no longer, so arranged to meet his river keeper, Fred Brown, there on the Lower Beat the next morning.

'He was always punctilious about soaking his gut casts over-night in a basin, but for some reason on this occasion forgot to do so. He therefore decided to start at the head of the pool, where there was seldom a fish, and let his cast soak as he moved down.

Major John Mills and the late Sir John Mills with some good fish at Bisterne in 1937

'He had only fished a few casts when his fly was taken. The fish came to the surface and rolled, giving both of them a good view of its great length and depth, before it bore down and broke the gut. Both Fred Brown and my father handled 40 pounders, but they mournfully agreed in later days that it was the largest fish by far which they had ever seen.

'This was in the spring. Three months later a very red fish of 45 lb was caught not far upstream, and my father always believed it was his fish, and that it would have topped the 50 lb mark when he lost it.'

The Bisterne Game Book in fact shows that a 45 pounder was taken on May 20th, 1904, by G. L. Polden on a gudgeon in a pool called 'Below Hurdles'. This was most probably the fish in question. It was described in the Game Book as being 'very red', and its length was 50 in., with a girth of 26 in. These measurements, coupled with its weight, give it a poor condition factor. According to Sturdy's scale of weight by measurement, a salmon of 50 in. length in good condition should weigh $53\frac{1}{2}$ lb.

The Hurdles pool was subsequently renamed 'Seven Acres', according to a note in Sir John's fishing diary, and it lies a few hundred yards upstream from the Lower Osier Bed.

Of course, there could be no absolute proof that both these fish were one and the same, but the evidence makes it seem likely.

As soon as he gained control of the fisheries at Winkton, Sir John voluntarily abolished river netting on that beat and at Bisterne, which had been spasmodically practised together with rod fishing up to that time. The Bisterne Game Record Book describes for instance the following intermittent net catches:

1892: Avon Tyrrell—16 salmon of an average weight of 18 lb.
      Bisterne   —59 salmon of an average weight of 21 lb.
1893: Avon Tyrrel —8 salmon averaging 23 lb.
      Bisterne   —14 salmon averaging 24 lb.
1894: Bisterne   —7 salmon averaging 23 lb.

Other net catches are not recorded, but it is interesting to note that in the 1890's net fishing in these non-tidal waters was obviously perfectly legal.

Sir John was also instrumental in bringing to a close the net fishing at the Royalty in 1920. There is an entry in his fishing record book under that year: 'This was the 1st year the nets at the Royalty were off'. Such closing down of net fishing was of course an immense benefit to rod fishing, as can easily be appreciated.

He was a member of the Hampshire River Board from around 1908 to 1946, and Chairman of it for many years. Subsequently, when the Avon and Dorset Fishery Board was formed, he was a member of that body until the formation of the River Authority in 1963. During all these years he never ceased to work for the benefit of the Avon and Stour fisheries—for instance he was largely responsible both for the construction of the new fish pass at Throop on the Stour in the early 1930's, and for the improvement to the fish pass at Ringwood on the Avon at the same time. The latter, although still not perfect, at once enabled fish to travel more freely upstream, and made Somerley a salmon fishery of note when it had previously been considered negligible in this respect.

All Avon fishermen owe Sir John a debt of deep gratitude and should revere his memory.

A brief record of Bisterne rod catches since 1902 may be of interest. So far at least as weights of fish are concerned, it is no doubt typical of most other Avon fisheries:

Year	Average Yearly Bag	Average Weight	Highest Year's Bag
1902–1911	13	23 lb	30
1912–1921	42	22 lb	60
1922–1931	50	22 lb	105
1932–1941	64	22 lb	135
1942–1951	39	21 lb	86
1952–1961	59	18 lb	125
1962–1971	50	17 lb	94
1971–1982	24	15 lb	38
1983	41	12 lb	
1984	30	13 lb	
1985	59	14 lb	

N.B. The reduction in Bisterne catches since 1971 is mainly due to fish passing more quickly upriver, and pausing less frequently in the Bisterne water. It does not necessarily indicate fewer fish in the river as a whole, though this too could partly be the cause.

As regards the Bisterne fishing, the following recollections of the late Mr. Percy Brown, who was river keeper in addition to being gamekeeper there from the early 1920s to 1977, may be of interest. They run as follows:

> During my early days connected with salmon fishing it was nearly all spring-run fish, with an average rarely below 21 lb. We considered the season over by the end of May or early June; for one thing the river by that time was full of weed, and the fish were getting stale, not interested in lures. Now there is usually a summer run, and the season can go on to the end of July, even

Lord Tryon (the present Lord Tryon's grandfather) and Mr. Neville Chamberlain (Prime Minister) at Bisterne in the late thirties

later for beats in the upper parts of the river; weed is not so much of a problem now.

When Major Mills had any close friends fishing, it was usually my job to ghillie for them. On two occasions I had Mr. Neville Chamberlain, the then Prime Minister, to look after. Seeing him use a light rod, greased line and small fly, the first time I had seen it used, I thought we had a poor chance of getting a fish. However we had only been on the first pool a short time before we had a $19\frac{1}{2}$ lb fish on; after a reasonable time we had it on the bank. The same day Major Mills was looking after Major Tryon, the Postmaster General, and Sir John Burnett-Stuart on another beat. Major Tryon had two fish of 22 and 33 lb and Sir John one of 23 lb, so four fish for the day was quite good.

On another day three years later (in 1939), we were out again with the Prime Minister; this time we had a fish of $16\frac{1}{2}$ lb. I also saw two fish follow his fly within a foot, but they would not take, in spite of trying different flies. He would not use a spinning rod. Almost Sir John Mills' (as he then was) last words to me were:—'Do you remember when I made you gaff the fish for the Prime Minister, as I was too nervous to do it?

On the Upper Water at Bisterne

During the light evenings Major Mills would often come down about four o'clock and fish till about 7.30 pm, in which case he would leave word with my wife, asking me to join him when I had finished tea. On one occasion when I joined him, he had one fish on the bank and another on, which I later gaffed for him. He looked at his watch and said:—'You take the fish on, I'll catch you up, there's time for just a few more casts.' It was a good half mile back to my house; I had just got there when I heard him shout again, so back I went and gaffed that one. The same story again:—'A few more casts and I'll caltch you up.' I had nearly got home when the shouting started again, so I got down there and gaffed that one. This happened in less than eighty yards of bank, one long pool, the Hut Pool on the Middle Beat.

Our best season was in 1935 with a total of 135 fish, the average weight 22.4 lb, with 17 fish caught in February. A number of pools which produced fish in those days are now no good, such as Knobs and Golden Osiers.

There is no doubt that the Middle Beat is really favourite, and in those days the Hut Pool, High Harbour, and Upper Reach were a good bet. Some of the pools got spoilt by the river altering course, such as corners growing out caus-ing backwaters and no flow of water. I remember Sir Richard Glyn having a fish on in the tail of White Hole, which went downstream, and he could not follow for withy bushes. He cut his line, tied on a piece of stick and was lucky enough to gather it at the far end, and so killed his fish; now there is about 15 feet between bushes and river bank.

Mrs. Shawe caught the heaviest fish on the Bisterne water, 48 lb in 1936. It was hooked at the Knobs, and as I was given to understand gaffed after nearly three hours opposite the Lower Fish Hut. She was only using a very light rod. There were so many good fishermen that it would be difficult to place any one of them as best. The most fish to one rod in a day were Mr. Dew's eight fish; Mr. Cassey and his friend Mr. Scivier had twelve off the Middle Beat, but that was two rods. One rather interesting point, there were three rods from Dorset who took a day's fishing, and Major Mills asked me to go and look at them occasionally, as in those days the Top and Middle Beats were in one, and only two rods allowed to spin. They went away that night with six fish, total weight $151\frac{1}{2}$ lb.

Major John Mills with his 41 pounder at Bisterne

The Royalty Fishery

Four miles downstream of Bisterne, the Royalty water at Christchurch provides without doubt the best and most consistent fishing on the whole river. It is the bottom-most beat, and the highest tides affect it as far up as its two main weirs, the Great Weir and the Knapp Mill weir.

The total length of this fishery is around three quarters of a mile, on both banks; and it has two sets of hatches on it (apart from subsidiary flood hatches), one at the Great Weir, which takes most of the stream when the river is at spring level, and one lower down at Knapp Mill opening on to the well-known Parlour pool, which takes most of the reduced stream in summer. Both these sets of hatches are provided with up to date fish ladders, so that salmon can pass freely upstream whenever they want to do so.

The 'Parlour' on the Royalty water

Reference has already been made at the start of this chapter to the history of this fishery during the 19th Century, dating back as far as 1814, and perhaps it may be of interest to readers if some account is given of further developments in the 1920's which led up to the situation as it now stands.

Up to February, 1920, the Royalty water was in the hands of Miss Mills of Bisterne, who was the cousin of Sir John Mills, referred to above. In that month Miss Mills granted a 21 year lease of the fishery to a combination of upriver owners at a rent of £600 per annum. A condition attached to this lease was 'that the netting should be formally carried out annually'. In fact this meant, owing to the words 'formally' and 'annually' that the netting was effectively abolished, largely owing to the influence and efforts of Sir John Mills.

The above development was subsequent to a Memorial drawn up in August, 1918 by the Board of Conservators of the Hampshire Rivers Fisheries District, and afterwards presented to the Ministry of Fisheries. This document, a copy of which is still in possession of Major John Mills of Bisterne, makes interesting reading. After outlining the position of the two main weirs at the Royalty, and in particular of the 'Fishing Mill Dam' or 'Great Weir', the Memorial makes clear that it recognizes the Fishing Mill Dam as legalized by a Certificate dated 25th February, 1871, in the following words: 'The Fishing Mill Dam is legal in the following respect, that is to say that the use of a draft net in the pool at and below the Great Weir in combination with the racks and hatches forming part of such Great Weir is legal'.

The Memorial continues: 'The Pool is not fished with a draft net in *combination with* the racks and hatches as one process, which Counsel advises is the true meaning of the Certificate, but during the Fishing Season racks or gratings, through which no salmon can pass, are placed in every sluice at Monday noon and they remain in position until Saturday noon, and this is done generally throughout the Season, except for a short time when weed cutting is in progress and the racks must be taken out to allow passage for the weeds.

It will be seen that the river is blocked to ascending fish by reason of these racks, and the racks remain in position although no fishing may be taking place.

There is a properly constructed salmon ladder in the weir, but the ladder is rendered almost inoperative for the following reasons. The hatches are so lifted that the rush of water comes through two or more sluices fitted with the gratings, and as salmon when running make for the greatest push of water, they doubtless work up the current and are baffled and turned back by the gratings, so that the fish have little or no chance of finding the Ladder.

At times also the Ladder is inadequately supplied with water. It must be remembered that this is the condition of things throughout the fishing season, except for the weekly close time, so that comparatively few salmon can reach the spawning beds.

There can be little doubt that the Avon suffers from over-netting . . .'

In support of this finding the Memorial goes on to quote recent salmon catches as follows:

Caught by Angling above Knapp Weir	Royalty— Miss Mills' Net	The Run— Netting at the mouth of the Avon
1915: 92 salmon	599 salmon	658 salmon
1916: 106 salmon	452 salmon	385 salmon
1917: 88 salmon	566 salmon	472 salmon

It recommends by way of remedy:

  i. That no gratings should remain in the hatches unless netting is actually taking place.
 ii. That the hatches described as 'flood hatches' in the Certificate Plan should only be opened in time of flood, and no gratings or other obstructions should be placed in them.
iii. That an accurate return should be required of all salmon taken in the river.

This Memorial thus made plain in concise style the handicaps under which Avon salmon were suffering at the Royalty at that time (1918). As will have been seen from the figures of the Royalty net catches, these were pretty drastic, and Avon rod fishing suffered accordingly. If anyone nowadays complains that Avon salmon netting is too severe, let them think back to the situation before 1920 and be thankful!

The reaction of the Ministry to this Memorial is not certain, but it seems that an indirect result of it was that in February, 1929 Miss Mills sold the Royalty Fishery outright to the West Hampshire Water Company (the present owners), and simultaneously the combination of upriver owners who held the 21 year lease purchased for £3,000 the Royalty netting rights for salmon and sea-trout, covenanting at the same time never to exercise these rights, except that they had the right to net the tail race of Knapp Mill and to return fish so caught to the river above Knapp Mill.

The West Hampshire Water Company agreed to put in a proper fish pass at the Great Weir. This pass has since been improved and

The Great Weir on the Royalty water. The salmon ladder is on the right of the hatches

renovated. An efficient pass at Knapp Mill itself has also, since many years ago, been installed. This is at the head of the well known 'Parlour' hatch pool.

Ever since 1920 the Royalty has been exclusively fished by rod, which remains the situation up to the present date.

This fishery has a marked advantage over other Avon beats, in that it is only two and a half miles upstream from the mouth of the river at Mudeford, so that fresh fish out of the sea reach it very quickly. Most of them then pause, either in one of the two hatch pools or else in one of the many other holding places on the beat, and are apt to be good takers as the odds are that they have never previously seen either fly or bait. The size and type of fish are naturally exactly the same as elsewhere on the Avon, and it is recorded that up to the present time a substantial number of 40 pounders have been landed on the rod here. The biggest of these was Mr. G. M. Howard's fish of $49\frac{1}{2}$ lb caught on February 27th, 1951 in the Green Banks pool above the railway bridge. This fish also holds the weight record for the whole river to date. It is perhaps surprising, in view of the high average size of fish, that no salmon of 50 lb or over has ever been caught on the Avon; and in view of the present fall in the average size, it seems that the chances of meeting such an outsized one in the foreseeable future sadly are now remote. Even 30 pounders nowadays are none too common.

The Fishery Manager for the West Hampshire Water Company is Captain Peter Green, to whom the author of this book is indebted for much valuable information.

The Royalty is still fishing well, though as elsewhere on the river the average size of its fish has dropped by nearly half. Its catch for last season (1984) totalled 355 fish, averaging $9\frac{1}{2}$ lb, with its biggest fish 35 lb. It now averages 150 fish each year.

One further point in its favour should be emphasized. It produces a fair number of fish earlier in the season than any other beat on the river, being so close to the sea; even in February its normal catch is by no means negligible. Also its productive season is a long one, with fresh fish, smaller salmon or grilse after the heavier spring fish, being caught up to and as late as July. There is more chance of the visiting angler finding fresh fish here at any time in the season than on any other Avon fishery.

With a view to giving more chance to visiting fishermen, day rods for salmon on the Royalty have now been made available from July 6th when the regular rod season ceases, and certain productive pools are reserved for this purpose.

The lower reaches of the fishery, the Bridge Pool in particular, are renowned for their exceptionally good sea-trout fishing, where fish of 4 to 5 lb are not uncommon, and in the early part of the season, fish of 8 or 10 lb have been caught, and sometimes larger. (see p. 96).

Coarse fishing at the Royalty is probably as good or better than in most other rivers in the Country. Barbel up to 12 and 14 lb have been caught here and there is also excellent chub and roach fishing. It is true to say that this is one of the few rivers where salmon, sea-trout, and coarse fishing all flourish side by side, a remarkable situation. It would be difficult to discover a parallel elsewhere.

At the present time the chief hazards to Avon salmon, apart from the legal net and rod fishing efforts, are not difficult to assess. The first is illegal fishing by drift net at sea along the Dorset coast and possibly even along the Devonshire coast, which borders the salmons' migratory route. Undoubtedly such fishing is sporadically carried on and difficult to prevent, but its effects are not thought as yet to be unduly serious. Nearer home there is a fair amount of net poaching in the open sea close to Mudeford and also in Christchurch Harbour. The Wessex Water Authority and the West Hampshire Water Company between them do their best to check this, but such poaching is well organized and prevention is not easy. Further upstream in the river itself there is little illegal fishing, except at odd places where salmon gather, such as at the Wire Hatches in Salisbury. Here again the Water Authority bailiffs keep a constant watch.

A further danger, as already mentioned above (p. 101), occurs at some of the main fish farms on the middle or lower Avon. A number of salmon smolts, at the time of their downstream migration, are apt to get trapped against the metal screens at the inlet to fish stews, and to be held there by the water pressure, and so perish. At times too, particularly when the water is low, adult salmon have difficulty in passing upstream through the hatches at such places and congregate immediately downstream. The position in both cases is unsatisfactory; but the Water Authority hopes to take steps to deal with this situation.

Pike and coarse fish in general, of which there are so many in the Avon, are of course a permanent menace so far as young salmon up to the smolt stage are concerned. And it is surprising that the survival rate of young salmon up to that stage is as high as it is, considering that the Avon is so outstandingly prolific in coarse fish of all sorts. The same could be said in connection with brown trout, so plentiful in the upper river and tributaries. They prey hard on young salmon at all stages from ova to smolt—nevertheless the salmon still seem to survive.

Coarse fishermen, when using maggots as bait, are apt to catch a number of salmon parr all up and down the river below Salisbury; and however carefully these are handled, the consequences to them must often be fatal. But it would seem there is no practicable remedy for this, as coarse fishing on the Avon is as firmly established as salmon fishing, and coarse fishermen would be unwilling to give up the use of maggots or to increase the size of their maggot hooks which might prevent their catching parr.

In addition, there are naturally the manifold hazards of the salmon's sea life, including above all the recently arisen Greenland, Faroes and Ireland drift netting and long-lining, which twenty years ago barely existed. These do not menace the Avon salmon to any higher extent than they do those of the Frome or many other British rivers; nevertheless they are no doubt partly responsible for the shortage of three and four sea-winter adult salmon, for which in times gone past the Avon and Frome were so famous, as well as reducing the numbers of the smaller two sea-winter fish.

Pollution on the Avon, as mentioned above, is at present well under control, and is not now a serious menace, although in general the pollution of English rivers caused by intensive farming methods has to be carefully watched, as spawning grounds can be seriously affected. There is a limited threat from birds such as cormorants, at present on the increase as well as on the protected list, also herons; but this is no new factor. Mink have become established along much of the course of the river, but it is difficult to see how they can do much harm to salmon stocks.

All in all, therefore, it might be said that Avon salmon in general do not have to face up to hazards greater than those on other English rivers, indeed in many respects they are by comparison fairly fortunate. The worst effects are probably due to poaching and predation by coarse fish, though no-one of course can estimate the loss directly caused by Greenland and High Seas fishing, or Irish drift nets. (It is on record that smolts tagged in the Avon have later been caught as grown fish off both Greenland and Ireland).

There would therefore seem to be fair hope for the future. The fish ladders which the Water Authority plans to build on the middle Avon should give better access to spawning grounds, and these alone if successfully completed should result in an increase in stock, other things being equal, during the next decade or so.

Sea-trout on the Avon

It is not generally known that the Avon has a large sea-trout run. The figures of catches shown below establish this beyond doubt. At the same time, although they are occasionally caught as far upstream as Somerley or higher, these fish as a rule do not run far upriver, and many prefer to spawn in the acid water streams from the New Forest heathland which join the main river in its lowest reaches. (A similar partiality is shown by the sea-trout of the Test, the majority of which prefer to spawn not in the main river, but up the Blackwater, a small acid water tributary from the New Forest, which runs in close to Testwood near its mouth.)

The result in the Avon is that sea-trout fishing is largely confined to the lowest beat on the river, the Royalty fishery, where the incoming fish are apt to congregate, and higher up the river it is of little account. The average size of Avon rod-caught sea-trout is around 2 lb, nevertheless much larger fish are frequently caught, sometimes up to double figures in weight. Only lately (1985) a huge fish of 17 lb 6 oz was taken at the Royalty. Most of these sea-trout are caught on bait, and the best fishing period is from mid-June to the end of July. The legal rod fishing season lasts from April 15th to October 31st.

Recent Avon sea-trout rod catches are recorded as follows:

1970: 511	1975:1737	1980:3389
1971: 548	1976: 207	1981:2336
1972: 496	1977: 591	1982:1518
1973: 256	1978:2371	1983:1631
1974: 559	1979:5477	1984: 903
		1985:1387

A number of sea-trout are also caught by the nets at Mudeford, though fewer than by rod. The average weight of 5 lb varies little

PLATE 6

Upper water at Bisterne. Avon Castle in the left background

John Ashley-Cooper on the Avon at Avon Tyrrell. Double Spey casting in a strong downstream wind

PLATE 7

Ibsley weir pool—oxygenates water in summer

Salmon netting in the 'Run' at Mudeford

from year to year. Recent net catches are as follows:

1982 : 863
1983 : 620
1984 : 469
1985 : 312

N.B. These catches would have included some Stour fish, and it would be impossible to distinguish these from the Avon fish, although they would probably be in a substantial minority.

The average weight of net-caught fish is higher than that of the rod-caught, because the smaller fish escape through the meshes of the net which are large enough in size to allow this. Also net fishing ceases at the end of July, while in August and thereafter sea-trout of smaller size continue to run, and some are caught by rod, thus reducing the overall average rod-caught weight. The legal net fishing season lasts from April 15th to July 31st.

The Avon below Christchurch Bridge, with Christchurch Priory in background. The best of the Royalty sea-trout water.

Avon Coarse Fishing

The Avon, from times long past, has always been one of the most renowned coarse fishing rivers in the whole of England. The earliest written description of English coarse fishing is perhaps that contained in the abbot Aelfric's 'Colloquy', written in Anglo-Saxon and Latin about the end of the tenth century, in which the fisherman describes his prey being of 'eels, pike, minnows, bull-heads, trout, lampreys, and whatever else swim the river'. Although there is no specific mention of the Avon in this 'Colloquy', one may be quite sure that the practice of fishing for coarse fish in this river, as well as elsewhere in England, was well established by that time. True there is no reference to a rod in The Colloquy, and most of the fishing was probably then done by net or trap; nevertheless hooks are mentioned, and with them the use must be assumed of a line, and possibly of a rod of sorts also, which in any case would soon have evolved with the passing of time.

Ever since those early days coarse fish have undoubtedly thrived in the Avon, though it was not until Victorian times, with the advent of railways as a quick means of transport, that this river's full potential as a mecca for coarse fishermen developed. From then up to the present day coarse fishermen from all over the country have foregathered on its waters. It is said that the present value of its coarse fisheries in financial terms, although it does not exceed that of the salmon fisheries, comes fairly close to it; and the Avon has a well-deserved reputation as a coarse fishing river of superb quality.

To perform well at coarse fishing undoubtedly entails great skill. As Howard Marshall says in his delightful book *Reflections on a River* (1967): 'There is a fascination in coarse fishing as compelling as any to be found in fly-fishing for trout. I would say that those who catch big roach on public waters are just as skilful as those who take big trout on the Test. And often they fish very much finer than the dry fly man.'

In present times roach and chub are the main quarry on the Avon, with barbel, dace and pike a close second, together with perch and sometimes grayling. Most of these fish are habitually present in all sections of the river from Salisbury down to Christchurch, a distance of about thirty miles, so there is an ample extent of water. Many different angling clubs own or rent fishing on this long stretch of river, from the Salisbury Angling Club at the top to the Christchurch Angling Club at the bottom. There is little difference in the quality of the fishing throughout this part of the river, though if one is forced to make a choice it might be conceded that the Royalty fishery is outstanding, certainly so far as roach and barbel are concerned.

Outsized specimen fish from the Avon form an impressive list as follows:

Barbel: 17 lb caught at Bisterne in the 1950s, but out of season and by a salmon fisher.

16 lb 1 oz caught at Somerley in 1960, but not claimed as a record, as it was foul-hooked.

15 lb caught at Somerley in 1984.

Chub: 8 lb 4 oz caught at Christchurch in December 1913.

8 lb caught on the Royalty fishery in 1964.

Dace: 1 lb 8 oz caught in September 1932.

Roach: 3 lb 10 oz caught in January 1953.

3 lb 6 oz caught at Bisterne in 1985.

Grayling: 4 lb 8 oz from the Wylye in 1885.

A fish of 4 lb 12 oz was netted from the Avon at Longford in the same year and was returned to the water.

Pike: 37 lb 8 oz caught in Spicknall's Hole at Fordingbridge in October 1944.

The coarse fishing season lasts, legally, from June 16th to March 15th each year—though on some beats it is restricted so as not to clash with the salmon fishing, e.g. at Somerley it is shortened to the period August 1st—January 31st.

The method of fishing for shoal fish is normally by trotting with a float, or by ledgering (usually with a swim-feeder); and fish caught (except barbel and pike) are normally kept alive in a keep net before being returned to the water at the end of the day, a procedure greatly to the benefit of stock preservation.

Coarse fish and grayling normally spawn during spring or early summer. Grayling spawn on gravel, but the eggs of most coarse fish are adhesive and are broadcast by the hen fish over weed or any form of water vegetation or sunken roots and sticks. Most types of fish prefer to spawn where there is a slight current; on the other hand bream and rudd prefer still water. All the eggs are not deposited simultaneously, but are shed in batches over three or four days, as they mature, and are fertilized by the cock fish immediately on being shed by the female. They are of course at constant risk from predators such as eels, fish of many sorts, and waterfowl. It may be of possible interest to readers if a digression is here made by giving an approximate indication of the number of eggs produced in annual spawning by some of the main types of British coarse fish. As will be seen, such fish are extremely prolific at spawning time, and the wastage of eggs for various reasons in a river such as the Avon is immense:

Perch. A 2 lb perch has been estimated to contain 30,000 eggs, and a 4 lb perch 100,000 eggs; but Frank Buckland recorded an exceptional case when a female perch of 3 lb 2 oz held as many as 155,620 eggs.

Common Carp. A hen fish of $16\frac{1}{2}$ lb is recorded as containing $5\frac{1}{2}$ lb of spawn numbering over 2 million eggs.

A common carp of 4 to 6 lb lays about 600,000 eggs to produce perhaps 8 adult fish. But carp, unlike most fish, only spawn at intervals and not annually.

Pike. A 35 lb hen fish (according to Frank Buckland, the famous zoologist and piscine authority) contained 600,000 eggs. Normally a hen pike sheds 10,000/18,000 eggs per lb of her weight.

Bream. An average sized bream of 2 to 3 lb contains 200,000/300,000 eggs.

Roach. A hen fish contains approximately 100,000 eggs per lb weight of the parent fish.

By comparison, an Atlantic salmon contains 700/800 eggs per lb weight of the parent fish, and a sea-trout or brown trout 800/1,000 eggs per lb weight of the parent fish.

There can be no surprise therefore at the number of coarse fish which a river such as the Avon, already well stocked, is capable of producing. But the story of Avon coarse fishing in recent years has been by no means altogether a path of roses. In the 1960s coarse fish populations everywhere on this river started a serious decline, which continued during the 1970's. Various theories have been put forward to account for this.

It was thought that the use of Dieldrin and D.D.T. in spray used by farmers (until it was banned in the 1960's) could well have had some adverse effect on the breeding process. For instance, in the case of roach during the 1950's and thereafter, it was noticed that, although a few big fish were caught, the shoals of young fish had virtually disappeared. Another idea was that excessive and wholesale weed cutting during the breeding season, by weed cutting boats instead of by the old fashioned chain scythe, caused a lot of spawn to be washed away and lost. This was the most popular theory. Some people too thought that the creation of large scale fish farms on the river, as at Standlynch and Bickton, exercised a harmful effect on coarse fish stocks; it has been discovered upon investigation for instance that coarse fish move on a migratory pattern up and'down-stream to a greater extent than has been previously realized, and a number of them are apt to be trapped against the inlet screens to fish stews and so killed by the pressure of water holding them there. On further investigation however this has only proved harmful to a limited degree to local stocks, and would not have been responsible by itself for such an overall deterioration as actually took place.

An alternative possibility is that the general decline has been due to a natural change in the life cycle of fish. This may well have been a possible cause in the case of individual species, but one would hardly have thought it could have covered a decline that was so wide-spread. No one in fact has yet produced a fully credible and overall explanation, but perhaps it was a combination of some or all of these adverse factors that produced such an unfortunate result. In any case during the past three years there have happily been signs of recovery, which is encouraging, although there is still a long way to go if the former high level is to be regained; and at the best this will take a considerable period of time.

The Somerley water immediately above Ringwood is one of the many good coarse fishing areas on the Avon, and the author is indebted to the late Mr. A. E. Wallace Tarry, Lord Normanton's Fishery Manager, for much information about this fishery, nearly five miles in length, including carriers, a summary of which is given below.

The main species making up the resident fish population at Somerley, as on most of the Avon as far upstream as Salisbury, are roach, dace, chub, barbel, pike, gudgeon, perch, and grayling. During the general decline in coarse fish stocks during the 1960's and 1970's Somerley suffered equally with other fisheries on the whole Avon, and this in spite of the fact that practically no weed cutting has been done on this particular fishery for the past ten or twelve years. (This would seem to weigh against the theory that excessive weed cutting is responsible for the general decline of coarse fish.) However, since 1984 roach shoals have been starting to show up again, particularly in the carriers.

During the late '60's and early '70's, chub became badly infected with red worm, and these fish were in poor condition. This trouble has righted itself in recent years, and all chub now caught are healthy. Stocks of them are reasonably plentiful.

The population of dace has been patchy, but these fish behave in a curious way—here today and gone tomorrow. Looking over Ellingham Bridge in 1984 one could see on one occasion a shoal of several thousand dace. They were there for forty eight hours, and then disappeared and were not seen again.

Barbel are to be found at Somerley, as well as upstream as far as Longford. They seem to increase in numbers each year, and run to a large size; the biggest recognized one at Somerley, weighing 15 lb, was taken last year, (1984). Its captor was not interested in claiming a record, and it was returned to the water after being weighed and witnessed by a companion. Another huge barbel of 16 lb 1 oz was caught at Ibsley on the Somerley water on March 6th, 1960. But this too was not claimed as a record fish, as it was foul-hooked, and its captor again was not interested.

Perch disappeared for a time, but are now starting to appear again intermittently. Grayling have been absent for years, but are now also tending to return, though in no great numbers. Newcomers to the water are bream, now to be found in several places, also carp. The latter are not abundant but can be seen in some of the bigger 'slacks'. Both are likely to have originated in stocked lakes or stews, or possibly from some pike fisher's live bait turned loose.

As to pike, here as elsewhere in the Avon these have always been fairly numerous, and liable to grow to a large size. The following anecdote, related by H. Cholmondeley Pennell in the Badminton Library volume on Coarse Fishing (1887), may be of amusement to readers who are not already familiar with it. It is headed 'The TAIL'.

'It was on the Hampshire Avon at Summerley' (sic), 'the beautiful seat of Lord Normanton, to whose courtesy I have been indebted for many a charming day's pike fishing, that the following incident occurred. My trusty friend, Mr. Darvall, with Lord Normanton's fisherman, Tizard, were paddling our way downstream in one of the small Avon punts, when we suddenly caught sight of the TAIL "broad as the baldrick of an Earl", gently undulating in an opening in the water-lilies.

The fish was evidently a huge one; the chance of tempting him to be caught "secundum artem" was nil. Tizard earnestly assured me his master was most anxious to have a large pike for the table . . . and so . . . I yielded to the tempter . . . The boat glides noiselessly down to the unconscious esox and now the gaff is stretched steadily but surely over the spot where the leviathan's shoulder is likely to be, giving him an imaginary length of about four feet . . . whish! There was a rapid stroke, a plunge, and with a rush sufficient to upset a whaleboat the stricken monster dashed for the bottom of the river, at that point at least twenty feet away.

It was an exciting moment. I found myself being incontinently pulled over the boat's side, which was taking in water freely, and clutching at the nearest available support, which happened to be the seat of the keeper's corduroy nether garments. It came away bodily in my grasp. At this juncture, nothing

I believe would have saved the boat from capsizing, if the gaff, yielding to the excessive strain, had not first twisted in the socket, and then straightened out, thus of course releasing the enemy who, though struck deep, may, I would fain hope, have yet survived in the indefensible attack upon him ''contra bonas mores'' and lived on to attain still greater age and yet vaster breadth of tail.

Tizard, the keeper, was the only one who did not laugh heartily, but on a hint that we should contribute to his next tailor's bill his countenance assumed its wonted serenity.'

Such monsters are not so often to be seen in the Avon nowadays, nevertheless the food for pike in the way of coarse fish is ample, and there would still seem to be little limit to the possible size which big specimens might attain. Incidentally, these outsized pike are always hen fish; the jack pike seldom reaches a weight of more than seven or eight pounds and is often devoured by the larger hen fish after spawning is completed.

In general there is no doubt that the miscellaneous fish population at Somerley is considerably below what it was twenty years ago. It does now seem however to be recovering from its worst level.

Another famous Avon coarse fishery is on the three mile stretch of river at Bisterne. The late Mr. Percy Brown, Major John Mills' retired head keeper, had this to say about the coarse fishing there in days gone by:

'I doubt if there could have been any better river for coarse fish in those days than the Avon. There were shoals of dace, roach, chub, perch, grayling, pike, a few brown trout, and the odd tench, though no barbel at that time. The heaviest pike on our part of the Avon was 30 lb, on a spoon fishing for salmon at Cottage Mead. Out of the same pool in another year Major Cornwallis-West had four pike of 28, 22, 19, and 15 lb.

During my summer holidays from school a Mr. Porter, a business man from London, rented the coarse fishing from the Boathouse up to the Avon Castle boundary, a distance of about $\frac{3}{4}$ mile. During August, when I was available, he would ask me to punt the boat for him while he fished for pike. He was very clever at that; using a single hook, he would lip-hook a dace, and hang a pear-shaped weight from a three-way swivel, which he called a paternoster tackle. His method was to cast across the stream, lift the rod, then let it sink, so that it looked as though the bait was in distress. There were so many pike in those days that it was not long before the bait was taken. The skill then was to know when the pike had turned the bait, so that with a single hook you did not just pull it out of the mouth.

My job was to hold the punt steady with the punt pole, no easy task for a twelve year old boy with a heavy punt in rather fast flowing water. The trouble was that he was good with a punt pole, and expected rather too much of me; however we got on very well.'

This is surely enough to show the past quality of the coarse fishing at Bisterne. Major John Mills, the present owner, says that roach and chub were the main quarry in those days, and that catches of over one hundredweight of roach to a single rod in a day were then on record. The decline in fish stocks in his opinion started during or soon after the 1939–45 war. Nowadays a catch of twenty pounds would be a good one. Incidentally Percy Brown retired from keepering in 1972, though he continued part-time working until 1977. He therefore witnessed the general decline of Avon coarse fish over these past thirty or so years, but had no firm opinion as to its cause. Bisterne has witnessed the same decline as other Avon beats, but as elsewhere is beginning to show signs of improvement during these last two years. A 3 lb 6 oz roach was caught there this year (1985), and returned to the water—not quite large enough to rival the 3 lb 10 oz of the record Avon roach caught in 1953, but not far off it.

Downton, Fordingbridge and Ringwood, as already mentioned, were all great coarse fishing centres. Howard Marshall, in his book *Reflections on a River*, describes a splendid catch of 60 lb of roach, five of them over 2 lb, on the Avon near Fordingbridge, together with a number of chub. Unfortunately however he does not give the date of this exploit.

Further downstream as already noted there is excellent coarse fishing to be had at Avon Tyrrell, at Winkton, and even better at the Royalty (see p. 93). The latter is particularly noted for its barbel, roach, and chub. It would be hard to find a better fishery or a more famous one anywhere in the country.

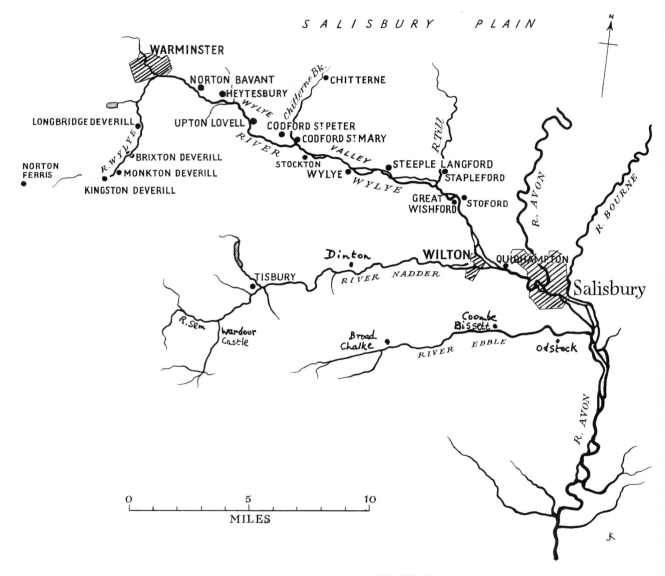

WYLYE, NADDER AND EBBLE

THE WYLYE

Of all the tributaries of the Avon, the Wylye is perhaps the most notable, with its clear sparkling water and enchanting valley from upstream of Warminster down to Wilton. A perfect example of an unspoilt chalk stream, flowing through delightful Wiltshire villages and countryside; what more could a keen dry fly man want? or anyone for that matter who delights in the natural charm of the Wessex landscape. Actually, to describe the Wylye as a tributary of the Avon strictly speaking is misplaced, as it joins the Nadder just below Wilton, and it is the latter river which carries on to the Avon at Salisbury after a further mile or two. So, to be exact, the Wylye is the Nadder's tributary rather than the Avon's, though there is only a short distance in it.

The two sizeable towns in the Wylye valley are Warminster and Wilton, and as mentioned above there are also a number of villages, the main ones being Norton Bavant, Heytesbury, Upton Lovell, Codford St. Mary, Wylye, Steeple Langford, Stapleford, Great Wishford and South Newton. The surrounding countryside is very obviously a downland chalk area with only a thin layer of earthy topsoil. In its natural state it would consist of rolling downland, far and wide. Now, thanks to the aid of artificial fertilizer, it has been made to yield crops, and is mostly cultivated. Along the river itself lie fertile water meadows, of the type to be found almost everywhere along south country chalk streams.

The uppermost reaches of the Wylye are known as 'The Deverill Brook'. The clear spring water of this stream comes welling out of the chalk subsoil close to the village of Norton Ferris, on the road between Mere and Frome. There is no doubt about its origin as a true chalk stream, fed subsequently by more riverbed springs.

This infant river, for the time being so small as to be hardly noticeable, flows for a short distance along hedgerows, then surreptitiously disappears underground for about one and a half miles, finally to emerge with an increased flow a short distance to the west of Kingston Deverill, another delightful and remote Wiltshire village. At Kingston Deverill a by-road crosses the Deverill Brook by a paved ford which is said to date from early AD, carrying a Roman road northwards towards Bath. The Deverill Brook here flows in a north-easterly direction, past Monkton Deverill, Brixton Deverill, and Hill Deverill with its handsome manor house and barn, all similar small villages of pleasing character. It finally reaches Longbridge Deverill, with its picturesque alms houses and Norman church, on the modern main road from Shaftesbury to Warminster.

Near Brixton Deverill there is a water abstraction point from a bore-hole close to the Brook. Fortunately, the amount of water subject to extraction is strictly limited, and in dry summer conditions compensation water is fed into the Brook. In this case, little or no harm is done, unlike in places elsewhere. Such bore-holes, and they are now becoming numerous, are an insidious menace to the flow of all chalk streams. Abstraction is apt to be increased, little by little, over the years, until the spring flow in summer is drastically attenuated. It is only a question of degree, and can become disastrous in time. (See pp. 127 and 165). Unfortunately more bore-holes in the Chitterne area are scheduled to start operating before long. It remains to be seen what effect this will have on the Wylye's flow, and whether adequate compensation water will be provided, if necessary. One can only hope for the best.

At Longbridge Deverill there is a sizeable trout farm, one of many in the Avon catchment area. While any fisherman must inevitably be anxious as to the possibility of disease spreading from such farms, where unnaturally large concentrations of fish are closely confined, this farm has to date proved innocuous, except for the recent escape of a large number of small rainbow trout into the river downstream,

Wylye dry fly water in peaceful surroundings

to the upset of trout fishing this past season (1984). The rods on one main fishery this season caught over a thousand of these undersized and unwanted trout, averaging nine inches in length.

Up to this point the Deverill Brook, although a crystal clear gravelly stream, has lacked sufficient volume to provide reasonable trout fishing. By the time it reaches Longbridge Deverill, however, this has changed. It now becomes known as the river Wylye, and has increased in size. Here is found the Longleat fishery of about two and a half miles in length, the uppermost of the first class Wylye dry fly fishings, which extend continuously over the whole twenty-two miles of river as far as Quidhampton, just downstream of Wilton. Wylye fishermen are indeed lucky to have at their disposal such a long stretch of well keepered and well managed perfect chalk stream water.

Below Longleat, the present main fisheries, in order, are the Sutton Veny Estate water (a fine stretch of the upper river, though the construction of the Warminster by-pass close by it is at present causing some anxiety), then the Norton Bavant water, the Piscatorial Society's water all the way from the weir above Heytesbury to Stockton, the Salisbury District Angling Club's beat below Stockton, Mr. D. H. Thomas' water at the Mill House, Stockton, and Lord Hugh Russell's water at Bathampton House, Wylye. Below this, the Ballington water extends as far as Steeple Langford, and the Wylye Fly Fishing Club's water from Steeple Langford to Little Wishford, while the Salisbury Angling Club has a short stretch on the left bank. Finally, the Wilton

A stretch on the Wylye

Fly Fishing Club leases from Lord Pembroke about six miles of water in the Great Wishford area, down as far as Wilton Park. This club was founded in 1901, and now has some forty members with an extensive waiting list; it provides as good fishing as anywhere on the Wylye. Detailed records of its activities have only been kept since 1950, when it had some fifteen members who caught on average about

100 trout each season. Now, keeping pace with the increased membership, the annual bag has risen to around 600 trout of an average weight of a little over 1 lb. Some stocking has been done with fry and yearlings to help maintain the catch. The club's best recorded trout weighed 7 lb 1 oz and was caught in 1953. A number of other fish of between 4 lb and 6 lb 14 oz have also been recorded.

Below this Lord Pembroke reserves water for his own use, as he does on the Nadder. With few exceptions, the above fisheries have

Lovely trout water on the Wylye

both banks throughout their length, which is always an advantage, particularly in these present days of intensive fishing. The river naturally increases in size in its lower reaches towards its junction with the Nadder, but it never attains more than comparatively modest dimensions. It is reinforced on its course by two minor tributaries, the Chitterne Brook and the Till which runs in at Stapleford, neither of them big enough to provide much fishing, except that the Till's lowest reaches hold a number of trout from time to time, also grayling. These two brooks however, although small, do produce a valuable augmentation of flow for the main Wylye, though for the most part their banks are rough and uncared for.

Most beats on the river are stocked annually to a greater or less extent with immature trout, allowed to grow to a keepable size before being killed. This ensures that the river is amply supplied with fish, and it is not unusual for the best waters to produce a kill of four hundred to six hundred brown trout of $\frac{3}{4}$ lb upwards in a season. In the lower reaches, fish of $2\frac{1}{2}$ lb to 3 lb or over are not uncommon, and stocking is carried out with sizeable fish. The Wylye Club for instance stocks its water with six hundred keepable trout each season.

Mills, and consequently mill-hatches, occur at frequent intervals all up and down the Wylye, a reminder of the former importance of water power at an early stage in production of daily bread. As on all chalk rivers, any hatch pool is always an attractive feature, providing a refuge for fish of all sizes, while the white water of the downward rush produces welcome oxygenation of the warm summer flow. During winter and early spring it is customary for hatches to be drawn fully open, so that there is little check to the stream. This allows the bed of the river to be cleansed of excessive mud and silt, and for the gravel almost everywhere to be washed clear. Weed growth, mainly of ranunculus, is consequently healthy; though ribbon weed, and in hot weather flannel weed can be tiresome.

Weed cutting on the Wylye, as on other chalk streams, plays an important part in river management. On the Wylye it is all done by hand during the recognized weed cutting periods of ten days at the end of April, three weeks at the end of June, and ten days at the end of August. The cut weed is allowed to float downriver, but as mentioned above the Wessex Water Authority's boom, inserted below Salisbury at weed cutting times, ensures that the vast majority of it is collected and there removed from the river, to avoid distrubance to anglers further downstream. This system now seems to

PLATE 8

Beaulieu Palace House

Harford Hole. A good pool on the Beaulieu river for sea-trout

PLATE 9

Stourhead gardens

Julian's Bridge over the Stour at Wimborne

A hatch on the Wylye

work efficiently.

Pollution is not at present a problem on the Wylye. There are occasional minor cases of it in the lower river, but insignificant in character and extent. Most of the river, fortunately, is completely pure.

Fly life is abundant, with mayfly now plentiful right up to the headwaters. Shrimp and snails are also prolific, but crayfish are in danger from the disease now spreading slowly upstream from the Avon. It seems likely that this breed of crustacean is doomed to extinction in the Wylye, a sad loss from all points of view, including that of the trout's menu. Lord Pembroke says that this disease unfortunately has now penetrated as far upstream as his water.

At the bottom end of the Wylye lies Wilton (a name no doubt derived from 'Wylye-ton), the ancient saxon capital of Wessex, which gave its name also to the county of Wiltshire. Wilton was an important local centre several hundred years before New Sarum was founded, and is situated on the banks of both Wylye and Nadder,

Wilton House

where originally there were fords until both streams in due course were spanned by bridges. Wilton now is a small though bustling country town, famous for the manufacture of carpets ever since the seventeenth century. Wilton House, the magnificent home of the Earls of Pembroke, with its splendid collection of pictures and furniture, stands amid delightful gardens in an extensive walled park with fine cedar trees. The original house was built by Sir William Herbert, about the year 1551, in the grounds of an abbey which had existed at Wilton for centuries earlier. This abbey was 'dissolved' by King Henry VIII, and its lands given to Sir William, created the first Earl of Pembroke, who subsequently built the original house at Wilton in the abbey grounds about the year 1551. The fourth Earl of Pembroke later had the formal garden constructed to the south of the house. Unfortunately, the original house was partly destroyed by fire in 1647, but was reconstructed by Inigo Jones and John Webb, and so remains to this present day.

The Wylye at Wilton

Before leaving the subject of the Wylye and its valley, some mention should be made of intruders amongst its trout stocks, i.e. coarse fish. Coarse fish are remarkably few, considering the close proximity of the main Avon in which, below Salisbury, they abound. Pike are always a hazard, more so in the lower reaches than headwaters, though they have been known to penetrate as far upstream as the Sutton Veny water. They are however rigorously kept down by trapping and netting as well as by periodic electric fishing. They are not allowed to appear in any substantial number.

Grayling have always been potentially plentiful in the lower half of the Wylye, as in other neighbouring rivers; though they seldom arrive in the headwaters, preferring the middle and lower reaches. They are looked upon with mixed feelings, either as vermin better removed from competition with the trout, or as a source of autumn or winter dry-fly or nymph fishing for those who are keen to pursue this form of sport, which can be good fun given reasonable weather.

If left unchecked grayling are most prolific, and this is the main drawback to their presence in trout water. When spawning a hen fish of 1½ lb can shed as many as 4000/5000 eggs, and although many of these are not fertilized or are destroyed in one way or another, sufficient remain to produce a good survival. Spawning takes place in late March and April, and there is no true pairing of spawners, they seem to prefer spawning in shoals which may be another reason for their prolificacy.

There is no doubt that the food which adult grayling eat is in all respects almost identical with trout food, and they are quicker on the whole to seize food than are trout, perhaps owing to their having keener eyesight. The result is that trout by degrees are apt to be driven off the good feeding areas. It is thus true to say that if present in sufficient numbers grayling will go far towards crowding the trout out. There is also little doubt that large grayling are predatory and will eat small fish such as minnows, bullheads, loach, and probably trout fry and yearlings during the winter months. Fish of 2 lb or over are undoubtedly more inclined to become bottom feeders, and less ready to rise to surface food.

The above are the main reasons for at least keeping their numbers under control in a trout water. As Frank Sawyer remarked with regard to the Upper Avon: 'I have often cursed whoever introduced grayling into a river which, in its upper reaches, is so ideally suited for producing first class trout and, what is more, for producing the multitude of insects which play such a big part in dry-fly trout fishing.' The same dictum might fairly apply in the case of other trout rivers in the neighbourhood.

Most fishermen would agree (though perhaps not quite unanimously) that as a sporting fish the grayling is not comparable to the trout. On the other hand grayling fight well on light dry-fly tackle. They are apt to rise quickly to the fly and directly from the river bed, unlike trout, no matter what the depth of water; and the actual rise-form is similar to that of a trout, it often being difficult to distinguish between the two. They do also provide back-end sport after the end of the trout season, even in cold weather. A day's good grayling fishing, which may provide as many as half a dozen fish or more averaging $1\frac{1}{2}$ lb is something well worth remembering, and grayling are good takers on the right day. These are the reasons why in some areas they are tolerated; but as Frank Sawyer again remarks: 'If preference is to be given to trout then the grayling must be checked, so that they cannot outnumber them.' He also points out that once they are established it is impossible to get rid of the grayling altogether.

From a culinary point of view once more it will generally be agreed that grayling do not come up to the standard of trout (or at least of wild trout). But it must be remembered that after their spawning in the spring they have not fully recovered to first class condition until the autumn, and it is only then or during the winter that they should appear on the table. If well cooked they are then at least reasonable, if not 'cordon bleu.'

As to size, 1 lb to $1\frac{1}{2}$ lb is about normal, anything over 2 lb is a good fish, and 3 lb a specimen one. The largest British grayling on record weighed 4 lb 12 oz, and it was netted from the Avon at Long-ford in 1885 and returned to the water. Dr. T. Sanctuary in that same year landed another large fish on the Wylye by fair angling and this weighed 4 lb 8 oz. Yet another fish of 4 lb 4 oz was caught on the Itchen, but such weights are indeed scarce.

As to the extent of their habitat, grayling are found in most of the English chalk rivers, at least in their middle or lower reaches; also in many rivers all over Britain, from the Tay and Tweed and other Scottish rivers right down to those of the south-country. They prefer everywhere the slower running streams rather than the rapid headwaters. They are also widespread in the countries of Western Europe, such as France, Belgium, Germany, Austria, Denmark and Sweden; so there is no scarcity of them. But in Ireland curiously enough they do not exist, having presumably never been introduced there.

Coarse fish in the Wylye such as dace, roach and chub seldom appear; and then only in the lower reaches.

Salmon occasionally are found in the Wilton area, though not often until the autumn. Lord Pembroke, who is a keen and proficient fisher-man, would welcome more of them during the fishing season. He sometimes catches some fish in the Wylye or Nadder during the late spring and summer, but there are hatches lower down the main Avon which delay their upstream passage. The Wessex Water Authority plans to build fish passes at these, so it is possible that salmon fishing in the Wilton area may improve in years to come.

Of vermin other than coarse fish, the worst are herons and the occasional cormorant—both a serious menace where trout fisheries are concerned. Though they are both protected birds, their numbers in places are extensive. Swans also can be a nuisance. They have lately congregated in numbers near Wilton, and can strip a section of river bare of weed if sufficiently numerous. Their presence in such large numbers constitutes a problem of some difficulty at this present moment. Howard Marshall in his *Reflections on a River* made some pointful observations on swans: 'Their glare seems to me to be not so much inquisitive as baleful, and as they steam over the very place where a big trout was rising, you can almost hear the parent birds saying to the cygnets, 'That's it, my dears, whenever you see a fisher-man make as much nuisance of yourselves as you possibly can'. Swans are beautiful creatures, no doubt, but I profoundly wish that the swan-uppers would come and remove mine to their swanneries'. There is nothing left to be added to this.

THE NADDER

The Nadder, especially when reinforced by the Wylye at Quid-hampton below Wilton, is the largest of the Avon's tributaries. This attractive river rises close to Donhead St. Mary and Donhead St. Andrew, near Shaftesbury and on the Wiltshire/Dorset borders. Its early course lies northwards, past Wardour Castle (where it is joined by a small tributary, the Sem), until it reaches Tisbury. Here its flow is increased by two further tributary brooks from the direction of Fonthill; and it now turns eastwards to flow past Teffont, Dinton, and Barford St. Martin. Growing all the time in size it eventually runs through the park of Wilton House, is joined by the Wylye at Quidhampton 350 yards downstream of Wilton Park wall, and finally, having completed a course of around 22 miles, divides for a short distance into two branches before uniting with the Avon close by Salisbury Cathedral Close.

In many ways, particularly with regard to the countryside and surroundings through which it flows, the Nadder is a close counter-part of its neighbour, the Wylye. But there is one significant dif-ference; the Nadder, unlike the Wylye, is not a true chalk stream. Greensands predominate on its upper course as far down as Dinton and Baverstock, i.e. over at least half of its length. Although it is joined by chalk-fed tributary brooks from Fonthill and Chilmark, and lower down from Teffont and Fovant, its water in its upper reaches is more acid than the pronounced alkaline of a true chalk river. As a result it lacks there the abundant weed growth of ranunculus, so typical of chalk streams, and its fly hatch is not so copious as it might be.

This however is only a minor drawback so far as fishing is con-cerned, even if it results in a slightly retarded rate of growth in wild trout; by and large the Nadder produces excellent trout fishing over most of its course, and its fame for this is widely recognized and appreciated.

The valley bed for the main part of this river's course is of clay, and its water colours quickly after rain which is apt to run off the top of the adjacent clay fields without becoming absorbed in the sub-soil. The result is that the Nadder often rises and colours more quickly than the purer chalk streams of the neighbourhood, also it falls more quickly. In winter heavy rain and sometimes melted snow are apt to cause floods, more so than in a true chalk stream, with consequent damage to banks and hatches. The river bed is mainly of silt, inter-spersed with gravel shallows, (used by trout for spawning though it is not thought that their natural regeneration is extensive).

These however, it should be emphasized again, are all com-paratively minor drawbacks. The greensand origin together with the predominantly clay valley bed in no way diminish the allure of the Nadder's surroundings. On both sides, though particularly to the south, there are high chalk downlands, sometimes cultivated and sometimes still under grass, so typical of this part of Wiltshire. Along-side the river there are water meadows with their carriers and 'drawns', and with mills and hatches at intervals, just as along the Wylye or the upper Avon. The valley is peaceful and unspoilt, and the river well clear of main roads and consequent traffic; the railway line from Salisbury to Exeter, it is true, runs close alongside much of the Nadder, but trains are not too frequent. It is a beautiful and restful valley, while in its lower reaches the magnificent grounds of Wilton House, together with the Palladian Bridge over the river, form an additional enhancement to its attractions.

Turning to the wildlife of the Nadder valley, whether relating to the animal, bird, or insect world, this as might be expected is abund-ant. To start with the river's fly life, so important to anglers—this is reasonably plentiful, even if perhaps not quite so prolific as it would be in a true chalk river. Mayfly appear every year during the latter half of May and early June, together with olives throughout the season. (Some of the heaviest hatches of mayfly on the lower Nadder, curiously enough now appear as late as August or thereafter.) Black gnats are also common; and in the early part of the fishing season grannom, iron blues, and March browns are to be found at

Palladian Bridge at Wilton over the Nadder

frequent intervals. Later on pale wateries, B.W.O., and sedges in the evening show up from time to time. July and August are apt to be bad months as far as fly hatches are concerned, with the evening the best time for fishing, though the evening rise does not often last for long.

September is a better month, when Daddy Long Legs can appear in numbers, and are greedily preyed upon by the trout. Small fly also again become more abundant during this month.

Underwater feed is fairly plentiful, though not so prolific as it might be if the water were more purely alkaline. It consists chiefly of snail and shrimp, together with adolescent crayfish. Whether in the future these latter are destined to succumb to the crayfish disease now prevalent in the main Avon remains to be seen; apparently they are already defunct in the Nadder as far as upstream as Wilton, which seems ominous. This disease is said to move upstream at the rate of about two to three miles per year, and is 100% fatal. It will be sad if crayfish disappear altogether here, and one can only hope for the best.

Riverside birds are as varied and numerous as along any other river in this neighbourhood. Mallard are common, with other sorts of duck and waterfowl. Snipe arrive from time to time, a few of them remaining throughout the year. Herons, though unwelcome visitors, are to be found not infrequently, and swans at nesting time continue after their usual manner to dispute the right of access along the banks. Kingfishers are also to be seen intermittently. In fact all the normal hierarchy of riverside bird life is well established in this valley, a source of endless interest and entertainment.

As regards animal life, otters were formerly not uncommon; but as elsewhere sad to say they seem lately to have become virtually extinct. Water voles, unwelcome for their tiresome bank excavations, are plentiful. Mink, as on most rivers, have arrived in recent years. They are nothing but a pest, and are wholly unwelcome. Fortunately they are not yet numerous along the Nadder, but are a latent menace, being extremely prolific breeders, and apart from mankind are threatened by no hostile animal or bird predators, which might keep their numbers in check.

Pike are something of a problem in the lower Nadder. They are netted inside Wilton Park every year, and the water below the park was electro-fished in the autumn of 1984, when 35 sizeable pike were removed. There is of course nothing to stop pike and other coarse fish ascending the Nadder from the Avon, and no doubt many do so. The only answer is to keep their numbers in check by methods such as the above. At present it is only in the lower half of the river below Dinton that they occur to any extent. Above that they are scarce, if not for the time being extinct.

Grayling, roach, and dace occur in increasing numbers as one travels further downstream, past Quidhampton to the junction with the Avon. This in the circumstances is only to be expected, but two mill hatches in the lower Nadder below Quidhampton check their upstream passage.

Salmon appear in the Nadder as they do in the Wylye (see p. 117). In a high water year odd fish are to be found in the lowest part of the river during the fishing season, and a few are caught upstream as far as Wilton. In a low water year however they seldom succeed in passing through various hatches lower down on the main Avon until the autumn. In November or December a fair number are to be found spawning in the lower Nadder, at least as far upstream as Barford St. Martin, as has been the case for many years past (as well as in the lower Wylye). It is possible that the salmon fishing on the lower Nadder could be greatly bettered if more fish passes were built (or improved) at obstructions on the main Avon below. It is to be hoped that this may before long be accomplished, so that these fish may arrive in large numbers during the fishing season. It is unlikely however that they would permeate far up either Nadder or Wylye except possibly in limited numbers during the spawning season, as the stream in both cases quickly becomes too small to give them adequate shelter.

There are several extensive and well-organized fisheries on the Nadder. The uppermost one is the well-known Teffont Fishing Club, which has about 4 miles of water on both banks from Lower Chicks-grove down to half a mile above Dinton Mill. This club was founded as long ago as 1913 by a small syndicate. By 1923 its membership had increased to sixteen, and by 1947 to twenty. Since then more members have gradually been recruited, to a total lately of thirty-four, with three additional honorary members, to which can be added an extensive waiting list. This fishery is well and efficiently managed, and well keepered. Its water has been netted almost every year, which has eliminated pike and keeps other unwanted fish well under control. Weed cutting is efficiently organized, and banks and foot-bridges well maintained. Since 1922 the Club, having decided that wild fish alone were not sufficiently numerous to produce the required bag, has every year stocked its waters to a greater or less extent, usually with brown trout fry in varying numbers from 11,000 to 75,000, and more lately with 300 or more yearlings of seven to eight inches in length. Rainbow trout of a keepable size (averaging

River Nadder. Fourteen Hatches at Wilton

between 1 lb–1 lb 8 oz) have also been introduced in comparatively small numbers over these past fifteen years to provide additional sport during the normally dull months of July and August. This policy has produced over the past twenty-five seasons a yearly normal bag of 500 brown trout, averaging in weight just over 13 ounces, with the biggest fish anything up to $2\frac{3}{4}$ lb. In addition, the yearly bag of rainbow trout amounts normally to about 150 fish averaging $1\frac{1}{2}$ lb, and running up to $2\frac{3}{4}$ lb in the case of the biggest. Grayling are also to be caught by those who enjoy fishing for them, and more than 100 of these, over and above the victims of the net-fishing, are usually accounted for by rod each year.

The Teffont Fishing Club has obviously kept to the principle that, so far as brown trout are concerned, wild fish or at least fish with a wild adolescence are preferable to stew-reared fish introduced into the river at an already keepable size. There is much to be said for this, if it can be well managed. Undoubtedly this Club's water provides a happy hunting ground for any discerning dry fly fisherman who is not overwhelmingly ambitious to capture specimen fish.

On the Lower Nadder, below the Teffont Club's water, there are a number of excellent fisheries. The first is Mr. Newman's water at Compton Chamberlayne, well keepered and well stocked with sizeable brown trout and rainbows. Specimen fish are caught here every season.

Below this lies the Burcombe Club water, managed by Major Perkins, and further downstream still Lord Pembroke reserves about one mile of first class fishing within Wilton Park. Just downstream of the main road bridge alongside the Park wall and about three hundred yards above the junction of Wylye with Nadder lies Fourteen Hatches, the upstream boundary of the Quidhampton fishing under the control of Mr. D. A. Nickol, to whom the author is indebted for much useful information about both Nadder and Wylye. This is the lowest downstream trout fishery on the Nadder, and it extends to about three quarters of a mile below the junction of Wylye and Nadder as far as Lower Bemerton, below which two successive mill hatches limit the upstream passage of fish. In this area in any case coarse fishing under the aegis of the Salisbury Angling Club largely takes over, also there are many grayling down here, as there are for that matter all the way up the Nadder except where they are rigorously kept down. They give fair sport in autumn and winter for those who are keen enough to fish for them. The Wessex Water Authority, as a matter of interest has transferred many grayling and coarse fish from the lower Nadder at Wilton where they are unwanted to the Avon at Salisbury where they are welcome.

All this part of the lower Nadder differs appreciably from the upper river belonging to the Teffont Club. Naturally the stream gradually increases in size until with the influx of the Wylye it has the flow and depth of a good sized river, as big as the main Avon upstream of Salisbury. And, in addition, in the bottom half of its course it assumes more and more the character of a true chalk stream, doubtless owing to the influx of chalk springs and feeders, which it tends to lack in its upper reaches. In this way it resembles in character the upper part of the main Avon.

Ranunculus grows reasonably well, and weed growth in general is prolific. There is however a pondweed designated 'potamogeton densus' which in places grows up thickly on the lower river and is apt to cause trouble by blocking the channel and smothering good weed. It is difficult to deal with it, as besides its being so dense the river channel is too deep to allow wading for weed cutting purposes. Weed cutting on the Nadder, incidentally, is all done by riparian or fishery owners, in accordance as usual with the overall cutting programme at specified dates.

The Quidhampton fishery is stocked yearly with two hundred or so keepable trout, which augments the naturally grown wild stock. Natural regeneration in this lower part of the river is not so prolific as might be desired, and wild-bred trout seldom seem to exceed 1 lb in weight. It has therefore been found necessary to introduce stock fish to provide an adequate bag. The upper part of the Quidhampton fishing as a matter of interest is by far the best. Below the Wylye mouth the river nearly doubles in size and becomes stronger and deeper. It is also apt to be somewhat choked in late summer by the pond weed mentioned above, and being close to Salisbury it suffers from sporadic poaching, an ever-recurring problem. As a whole therefore this lower stretch at Quidhampton is apt to be comparatively unrewarding.

There is some pollution even if not serious on the lower Nadder, mostly from farm sewage and agricultural spray. It is difficult to say how much harm this does to the fly hatch, though in other ways there is little evidence of damage.

To sum up, the Nadder taken as a whole is a charming river providing first class fishing over nearly all its length. Those who live on it and fish on it are indeed fortunate.

RIVER BOURNE

This tributary of the Avon is the smallest of the four which join the main river near Salisbury. In its upper reaches it is a winter bourne which in former days rose near Newton Toney, some nine miles north east of Salisbury to enter the main river just below Laverstock and a short distance downstream from the city; but nowadays it seldom appears far upstream of Porton. It is a true chalk stream, which in the past held a good head of trout, running up to 2 lb. It is a pretty little river, and up to twenty or so years ago used to provide good sport for the members of the Figsbury Fly Fishers Club, and others.

Such happy days now, alas!, are gone. The main trouble, so it appears, is due to water abstraction by bore hole, which results in a diminished flow, a severe handicap to any form of fishing. Dilapidation of hatches has also caused a fall in water levels. Only the bottom

six miles of the Bourne's fifteen miles or so full length still provide reasonable fishing. Near Winterbourne Gunner where the water height is maintained by use of a hatch there is still a fair head of trout, and below this the Salisbury Angling Club fishes the lowest part of the river, which is also productive. The Bourne also harbours salmon at spawning time within a mile or two of its entry into the main Avon. There are also a fair number of coarse fish of different species in this part of the river, together with some pike; but grayling outnumber all other types of fish, and are here noticeably prolific, more so for instance than in the Nadder or Wylye.

Upstream of Winterbourne Gunner however, little fishing is now done; and the upper part of the Bourne affords another sad example of how the fishing in a chalk stream can succumb to the demands of modern civilization.

THE EBBLE

After the Nadder and Wylye, the next most sizeable tributary of the Avon is the Ebble, sometimes known as the Chalke River. Its uppermost springs lie close to Alvediston, a remote Wiltshire downland village, seven miles due east of Shaftesbury; and the course of this pure chalk stream lies at its start through Ebbesbourne Wake and eastwards towards Broadchalke. The headwaters of the Ebble are, however, a winter bourne, a not uncommon feature of chalk streams; that is to say that although in winter and spring, when the uppermost springs break, there is a fair flow of water from the highest source, in summer this flow dries up, and in the case of the Ebble a constant flow only begins lower down near Broadchalke, where there are watercress beds and permanent springs. Other winter bournes follow a similar pattern.

After Broadchalke the stream descends to Bishopstone and the oddly named village of Stratford Tony. If anyone queries the origin of this name, the explanation is a simple one: it was where the Roman road, the Strata or Via Strata (the paved way) from Old Sarum (Sorbiodunum) forded the Ebble en route for Badbury Rings, near Wimborne, and then for Dorchester. This was part of the main road from London to Exeter. The suffix 'Tony' refers almost certainly to one of the Roman 'Antonine' emperors, either (and most likely) to Antoninus Pius, who reigned from AD 138 to 161; or else possibly to Antoninus Caracalla, who actually visited Britain on campaign with his father, Septimius Severus, before returning to Rome to become Emperor in 211. This road was without doubt made under the direct instructions of one of them, or at least under his aegis.

Below Stratford Tony the Ebble passes through the villages of Coombe Bissett and Odstock, and so into the main Avon near Bodenham, two miles below Salisbury. It is a very pretty small stream averaging 5 to 7 yards in width and a valuable feeder for the Avon. It holds trout throughout most of its course, certainly as far up as Bishopstone. The late Lord Head, although himself no fisherman, had some years ago accumulated a large number of these in his hatch pool there, and used to enjoy feeding them with pellets. Of course, the inevitable loss took place in due course, when after a winter's spawning season with some flooding nearly all these fish scattered to disperse elsewhere! But anywhere in these upper reaches, between Bishopstone and Coombe Bissett, a reasonably plentiful stock of moderate sized wild brown trout is to be found, averaging $\frac{1}{2}$ lb or so in weight, with a few bigger ones. Fishing up here is not easy; it demands a great skill and delicacy, coupled with the use of a very fine nylon leader.

All the best trout fishing on the Ebble, however, is downstream from Coombe Bissett. The river down here is immensely prolific in small trout, averaging between one half and three quarters of a pound. There is no need for stocking; the wild trout abound. A fish of one pound is a big one, and having reached that size they are inclined to 'go back'. Only in the bottom reaches of the Ebble at Odstock and below, where the fishing belongs to Lord Radnor, are bigger fish likely to be found. Down here there is always the chance of getting a much more sizeable one, especially if there is a mayfly hatch. Even a two or three pounder may have made his way up from the main Avon. The river here is also larger and deeper, averaging six to eight yards in width.

Later on, by November or after, salmon are sometimes to be found spawning in the lower Ebble which is a useful small stream for this purpose; although it never harbours these fish earlier on during the fishing season.

Coarse fish are not a problem anywhere in the Ebble except in the lowest reaches. It is only there that they occur, having permeated up from the Avon; roach, dace, pike, also grayling are to be found, but in no great number. Above Odstock, except for a few dace, they are absent.

Fly life on the lower part of the Ebble is plentiful. There is a fine hatch of olives throughout the season, also grannom, black gnat, and hawthorn in their time, with occasional iron blues. During the summer sedges, B.W.O., and pale wateries occur frequently. On the other hand, mayfly curiously enough are scarce above Odstock, and on some stretches apparently non-existent. This perhaps is no drawback. Shrimp and snails are also to be found.

Fortunately there is no large scale water abstraction from the Ebble, to reduce its natural flow, also very little pollution, only occasionally from minor sources. In the past some dredging to improve land drainage has been carried out on the lower half of the river, and with the demise of the water meadow system no less than six hatches have been taken out below Coombe Bissett. This has had the effect of lowering the water level in that area to a considerable extent, which no doubt accounts for the lack of larger wild trout, much of the river being now too shallow to hold them, which is a pity.

In conclusion nevertheless the Ebble remains a delightful and largely unspoilt chalk stream, giving great pleasure to those who are fortunate enough to fish it.

The Ebble near Homington in summer

THE BEAULIEU RIVER

Sea Trout Fishing

This small river is by no means a chalk stream, but nevertheless merits a mention in this book owing to its proximity to the Avon and in particular to its outstanding run of sea-trout.

It rises in the middle of the New Forest, near Lyndhurst, and after a southerly course of about eleven miles empties into the tideway at Beaulieu, and so out into the Solent after a further four miles of estuary. Its water has an acid content, derived from the New Forest peat through which it flows and which it drains. This type of water as noted elsewhere is particularly favoured by sea-trout.

The stream above the restricted tideway fishes for about $1\frac{1}{2}$ miles. North Gate marks the top boundary of this fishing, and Black Bridge near Beaulieu village the bottom boundary. There is unrestricted tidal flow up this river's estuary, from the Solent as far as the sluice gates near Beaulieu village. Above this the tide flows in, backing up the river to Harford Bridge about one mile upstream from Beaulieu, North Gate being still a further half mile upstream. The river's downward flow on the ebb-tide is then restricted to a minimum level by the sluice gates at Beaulieu swinging shut after high water. All the best fishing in this river is to be found in this stretch, where a good head of water is thus permanently, though artificially, maintained. Further upstream, above North Gate, fish do not penetrate until late in the season.

The river bed is not wide, about seven yards on average, and the flow is seldom if ever clear. It possesses a pronounced degree of murkiness, an advantage in that it makes day fishing as well as night fishing productive, an unusual benefit in a sea-trout water. The river also is sluggish as far upstream as Harford Bridge, but above that a delightful Forest stream. Harford Hole below this bridge is perhaps the likeliest catch, and a permanent holding place for fish. Elsewhere, wherever depth and shade combine, fish can be found.

'Fly only' is the rule on the Beaulieu River, and a single-handed rod is all that is required. The banks in many places are wooded, so that considerable dexterity is required in casting. Both dry and wet fly can be effective, and there is no wading beyond knee deep on occasion.

The legal fishing season is from May 1st to October 31st, but the best period is invariably from mid-June to the end of August, with the bigger fish being caught in June and July.

The average weight of the Beaulieu sea-trout is exceptionally heavy, as the following table of recent catches shows:

	Over $1\frac{1}{2}$ lb	$1\frac{1}{2}$ lb or less	6 lb or over	Average wt. over $1\frac{1}{2}$ lb	Biggest
1979	89	98	14	4 lb	$10\frac{1}{2}$ lb
1980	274	125	19	$3\frac{1}{2}$ lb	$9\frac{3}{4}$ lb
1981	473	62	67	4 lb	$12\frac{1}{4}$ lb
1982	145	8	44	5 lb	11 lb
1983	93	47	41	$5\frac{1}{2}$ lb	$10\frac{1}{4}$ lb
1984	93	95	17	$4\frac{1}{4}$ lb	$14\frac{1}{2}$ lb
1985	76	54	13	$4\frac{1}{4}$ lb	$8\frac{1}{2}$ lb

These fish have all been caught by not more than 3 rods fishing at a time. It is an impressive list, 1981 being a particularly good season. Although the bag fluctuates considerably, this is no more the case than on most other sea-trout rivers of note; while the weights speak for themselves.

As to other types of fish, salmon do not enter the Beaulieu River, and only a very occasional grilse has ever been caught in it. There are a few unwelcome rudd and perch to be found, also some bass in the tidal water. Mullet as in most south country rivers ascend it in numbers during the summer, but they are of no benefit for the angler. Eels of course proliferate here as elsewhere, and again are unwelcome.

Little netting is done. Two sweeps with a seine net are made every fortnight in the estuary, the main catch being of mullet, bass, flat fish, and eels. Sea-trout are seldom caught.

This river suffers little from flooding. Occasionally a very heavy thunderstorm in summer will raise and colour the water enough to put a stop to fishing for perhaps twenty-four hours, but this is a rare occurrence.

For anyone who is a reasonably skilful fly fisherman and who is prepared to take a fair amount of trouble over his fishing, the Beaulieu River offers fine scope for his efforts. (The best fishing times are normally during the first half of the morning, the late evening, or at night.) Of all the South-Country sea-trout rivers this one is probably the most sporting and the best fun to fish (even if owing to its small size it is not the most prolific). It appears to have suffered little if at all during the recent decades from that general scourge of our sea-trout, the vile U.D.N. And its catch, when it is remembered that this is made by three rods only and all on fly, whether for weights or numbers is indeed one of distinction.

Beaulieu Palace House

Beaulieu Palace House

Near the estuary of the Beaulieu River stands Beaulieu Palace House and Abbey, a Cistercian abbey and monastery being founded here by King John in 1204. His son King Henry III was present at its dedication in 1246. This monastery was 'dissolved' by King Henry VIII in the 1530's, and with the abbey is now largely in ruins. The Palace House, comprising what was originally the gate-house of the abbey but restored and enlarged, is now the home of Lord Montagu of Beaulieu, who in 1952 founded here his famous Motor Museum.

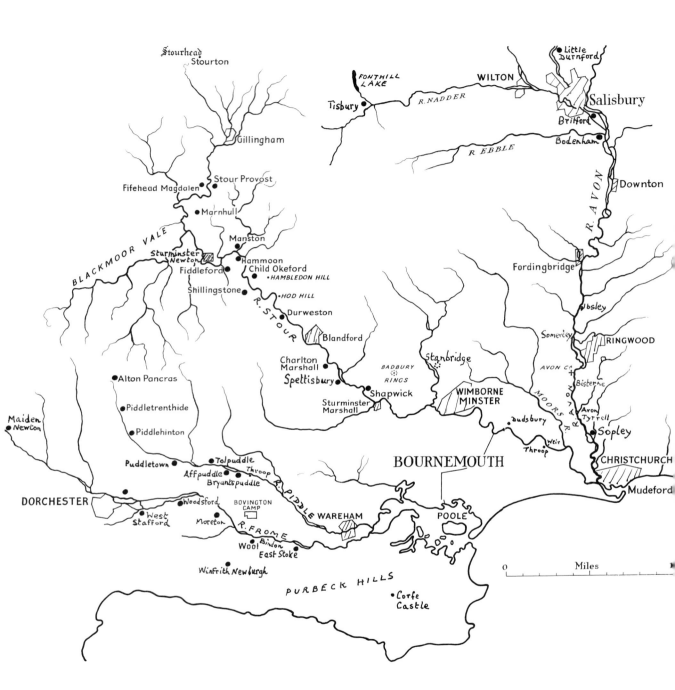

Stourhead
Stourton
FONTHILL
LAKE
WILTON
Little
Durnford
Tisbury
R.NADDER
Salisbury
Britford
Gillingham
R. EBBLE
Bodenham
Stour Provost
Downton
Fifehead Magdalen
R. AVON
Marnhull
Manston
BLACKMOOR VALE
Sturminster
Newton
Hammoon
Child Okeford
Fiddleford
Fordingbridge
HAMBLEDON HILL
Shillingstone
Ibsley
HOD HILL
R. STOUR
Durweston
Someriey
Blandford
RINGWOOD
AVON Cal
Charlton
Marshall
Stanbridge
Bisterne
Alton Pancras
BADBURY
RINGS
MOORS
AVON
R.
Spettisbury
Avon
Tyrrell
Piddletrenthide
Shapwick
WIMBORNE
MINSTER
Sopley
Maiden
Newton
Sturminster
Marshall
Piddlehinton
Dudsbury
Puddletown
Tolpuddle
CHRISTCHURCH
Throop
Throop
Weir
Affpuddle
BOURNEMOUTH
Bryantspuddle
PIDDLE
Mudeford
Woodsford
BOVINGTON
CAMP
DORCHESTER
WAREHAM
POOLE
West
Stafford
Moreton
R. FROME
Bindon
Wool
East Stoke
0   Miles
Winfrith Newburgh
PURBECK HILLS
Corfe
Castle

STOUR, PIDDLE AND FROME

136

THE STOUR

Although its source and uppermost reaches lie in Wiltshire, the Stour can fairly be classed as a Dorset river. It enters that county two and a half miles below Stourhead, close to its source; and subsequently never leaves it. The name Stour is reputedly of Celtic origin, and appears in the Domesday Book as 'Sture' or 'Stur'. It is a common river name; there are at least four other Stours in England, in Suffolk, Kent, Worcestershire, and Warwickshire.

The Dorset Stour joins the Avon at Christchurch, just upstream of its mouth at Mudeford, after a course of some sixty-five miles. The total fall in its journey from Stourhead to Christchurch is one of approximately 598 feet, most of which occurs in the upper reaches. In the middle and lower reaches its average fall is one of only three and a half feet per mile. Its total catchment area is around 487 square miles. This makes it easily the biggest river in Dorset, though slightly less than the Hampshire Avon's 658 square miles.

Though its headwaters originate in a chalk area, only three miles crow flight from the source of the Deverill Brook which develops into the Wylye, (see p. 107), the Stour cannot by any stretch of the imagination be classed as a chalk river. Its slow meandering upper and middle course as far as Child Okeford (four miles below Sturminster Newton) lies through the heavy clay of the Blackmoor Vale, where it is reinforced by a number of tributaries of similar character. The most notable of these are as follows: the Shreen at Gillingham, the Lodden a short distance downstream, (both of which run in from the north-east); the combined Bow and Cale, the Caundle Brook, the Lydden, and the Divelish from the south and west; with the Fontmell and Manston Brooks from the north-east. In fact, the Stour has altogether a large number of tributaries, no less than forty eight, though many of them are too undersized to be of any significance. And although further downstream this river may run between high chalk uplands, such as Hod Hill and Hambledon Hill and the downlands around Badbury Rings, and be joined below Blandford by chalkstream tributaries such as the Tarrant Brook and the Allen, throughout its length it maintains the same slow and sluggish character.

Its water is normally pretty clear, at any rate in the upper reaches, though a slight cloudiness is apparent in it from time to time. After rain or with flood, however, it is apt to colour quickly, and for three or four days on end. The river bottom is interspersed with thick weed beds, and it usually consists of mud, silt, or sand, though gravel patches occasionally appear. In the deep pools by contrast, and in the stretches immediately upstream of mills, hatches or weirs, the

Water at a low level

water often remains clear of weed, and attains a considerable depth of up to twelve or fifteen feet.

The Stour is apt to flood in its upper reaches after heavy winter rainfalls, but such flooding nowadays is short-lived owing to the drainage operations of the Wessex Water Authority. It seldom lasts for more than three or four days, and is in fact worse in the middle reaches of the river near Blandford Forum or below.

In general therefore this river has a noticeably different character to that of the nearby Hampshire or Wiltshire Avon, slower flowing and rather less clear. It lacks any wide-spread gravel bottom and chalk stream character anywhere below its uppermost reaches, being tortuous throughout its length, and more prone to flood. It is interesting to note the difference, where the Stour finally joins the Avon, in the colour of the water in these two respective streams, the Stour's flow being as a rule more clouded, and slower to run clear, even

Upper Stour

in summer. So, although this river runs through a delightful countryside throughout its middle and upper reaches, its unruffled though circuitous course harmonizing with the peaceful tranquillity of an unspoilt Dorset background, the Stour has the character of a slow-running lowland waterway, in contrast to the many clearer and brisker flowing chalk streams of the neighbourhood. It is perhaps more akin to the steady and solidly flowing rivers of the Midlands.

There is nothing uninspiring however about the Stour's source and uppermost reaches. Its headwater stream, bubbling from the Wiltshire chalk downland, is at once dammed to form a series of lakes, enhancing the enchanting landscape garden of Stourhead, with its temples, grottoes, and stone bridges. Stourhead House and its gardens owe their existence to the inspiration of Henry Hoare (1677–1727) and more particularly to that of his son, also named Henry (1705–1785), the former being responsible for building the house, and the latter for laying out the gardens and damming the Stour. Both Hoares were partners in the famous Hoare's Bank, founded by Sir Richard Hoare, the first Henry's father in 1672. Stourhead is now the property of the National Trust, both house and garden being meticulously maintained. They are objects of great attraction to both neighbours and visitors alike.

The memorial inscription to the second Henry Hoare, raised in 1815, runs as follows:

'To the Happy Memory of Henry Hoare Esqr.
Who was the first to clothe the noble woods,
The wild and formerly uncultivated lands of this estate,
And to adorn it with its various edifices;
Who conducted these waters from their springs,
Bringing them into the Grotto of the Nymph,
And gathering them into their present spaciousness;
Who erected the temples
Of Apollo and Flora, and the Pantheon;
'Who placed here—
Having purchased it from the City of Bristol,
Where it formerly stood—
The old stone cross,
A celebrated monument of our English Kings;
And who directed to be set up,

On a hill, conspicuous from afar,
A tower in the honour of
Alfred,
The renowned King of the West Saxons.'

Alfred's Tower, referred to above, was of course the well-known structure rising 160 feet from a wooded ridge already 800 feet high. It stands close to Stourhead, but just over the Somerset border. A memorial inscription to King Alfred runs as follows:

'King Alfred. AD 879. On this summit erected his standard against Danish invaders. To him we owe the origin of Juries, the establishment of a Militia and the creation of a Naval Force.

Alfred, the light of a benighted age, was a philosopher and a Christian; the father of his people, and the founder of the English Monarchy and liberty.'

Shortly after leaving Wiltshire, the Stour passes through the small country town of Gillingham in north Dorset, below which it enters the Blackmoor Vale proper. Here its course, as noted above, becomes lingering and winding, and sometimes liable to flood.

The meadows on both its banks are difficult to drain and are suitable only for grazing, which makes dairy farming the most commonly practised undertaking in this neighbourhood. Of late years however fat cattle and sheep farming have also become popular. Villages which here lie on its banks, a short distance below Gillingham, are West Stour and East Stour, the latter being associated with the writer Henry Fielding, who lived and worked there for a number of years. The Stour then passes by Stour Provost and Fifehead Magdalen, and eighteen miles downstream of Gillingham it reaches the ancient town of Sturminster Newton. This is an agricultural centre of some importance, (although endowed with only a modest population of around 2500.). For many years it has boasted one of the biggest cattle markets in the country, particularly for the sale of calves. It also possesses a sizeable cheese factory, Sturminster Mill on the river here is a picturesque old building with hatches and fine mill pool. It is one of

Sturminster Mill

the few water mills in the country still working. The road bridge at Sturminster, with its six arches, dates from the 15th century, but nevertheless carries modern traffic. There are a number of similar bridges to this one in Dorset, Wiltshire and Hampshire, such as those at Wool, Holme Bridge, Wareham, Wimborne, Witchampton, Fordingbridge and Harnham (among others). All these date from the 15th, 16th or 17th century, (which seems to have been a great bridge-building era), or even earlier in the case of Harnham.

The Sturminster bridge carries an iron notice, dating from the time of King George IV and threatening transportation for life as the penalty for anyone convicted of damaging it. Similar notices are still to be found on other Dorset bridges, as at Durweston, Witchampton, and Wareham. These reflect the unrest in Wessex agricultural areas, and the general fear it engendered, during the 1820's and 1830's (see p. 173), and are an interesting legacy of the past.

A short distance downstream from Sturminster lies the picturesque

Inscription at Fiddleford Mill

village of Fiddleford, with another delightful mill of very ancient origin. The old mediaeval hall at this mill, a separate building, dates from the mid 14th century, when it was rebuilt by the Latimer family, whose *fleur de lys* still adorns its doorways. This hall contains some wonderful panelling, ancient stone fireplaces, and is supported structurally by a series of magnificent oak beams. It is separated from the now disused mill house, which formerly contained the mill wheel; but let into the wall of this mill house underneath the stone slats of the roof are two limestone slabs, set side by side and measuring roughly six feet across. Across these slabs is inscribed in ornate Elizabethan script:

OPERAM DEDI	—1556—	MEIS SUMPIS ALIENIS

He that wyll have anythynge don   Let him com fryndly he shallbe welcom
A frynd to the owner and enemy to no man   Pass here freely to com when they can
In the tale of troth I do allway professe   Myller be true Disgrace no thy vest
If falsehode appere the fault shall be thyne   And of sharp punishment think me not unkind
Therefore to be true yt shall thee behove   To please God chiefly that liveth above

The lettering of this inscription is still quite clear and legible, in spite of some deterioration due to weather and vandalism. It presumably reflects the moralizing of some 16th century miller, and is a wonderful inscribed heirloom of a past age.

In the 18th century Fiddleford Mill and cottages were used as a storage place for contraband. Smuggling was a popular and well-established pursuit in the southern counties of England at this time, and not least in Dorset. The distribution of smuggled goods from inland repositories such as Fiddleford Mill was widespread and well organized. Kipling's poem from 'Hal o' the Draft', (admittedly relevant to Sussex, but Dorset would have been quite as applicable), depicts vividly the shadowy atmosphere surrounding such activity:

'If you wake at midnight, and hear a horse's feet,
Don't go drawing back the blind, or looking in the street,
Them that asks no questions isn't told a lie—
Watch the wall, my darling, while the Gentlemen go by!

Five and twenty ponies,
Trotting through the dark—
Brandy for the Parson,
'Baccy for the Clerk;
Laces for a lady; letters for a spy,
And watch the wall, my darling, while the Gentlemen go by!

Widely prevalent also in Dorset and Wiltshire is the well-known story of the 'moonrakers', engaged in the contraband business, who were raking their smuggled casks of brandy out of a pond where they had been hidden, when the excisemen inadvertently appeared. 'We'm be raking for thet ther' owld cheese' was their explanation, referring to the full moon reflected in the water. The excisemen's response is not recorded!

In present days the cottages and hall at Fiddleford have been restored, and are in good order and a delight to the eye; though the mill, unlike Sturminster Mill, is no longer worked.

No description of the middle and upper Stour would be complete without some mention of Thomas Hardy, the famous Dorset writer who lived from 1840 to 1928 (see p. 184). Although born at Higher Bockhampton, near Dorchester, Hardy was greatly attached to the Blackmoor Vale and the Stour Valley. He bought a house overlooking the river at Sturminster Newton and brought his wife, Emma, to live there. He would frequently walk alongside the Stour and upstream as far as the village of Marnhull, some four miles distant. This village under the pseudonym of 'Marlott', appears in *Tess of the D'Urbervilles* as Tess's birthplace.

Another Dorset celebrity was the famous poet William Barnes (1801–1886), the son of a small farmer near Sturminster. This remarkable man was a highly educated scholar, familiar with Latin, Greek, French, German, Italian, Spanish, Welsh, and Arabic. He was in addition an astute mathematician, political economist, antiquarian, and playwright; he also obtained a divinity degree. Barnes lived almost all his life in Dorset. Brought up close to the Stour and within sight of Sturminster, he was devoted to the Dorset countryside, its inhabitants and way of life. His numerous poems were frequently in the Dorset dialect, which he epitomized as follows: 'a pure, ancient language, rich and expressive and as free from artificiality as the speech of a child. If the Court had not been moved to London, then the Speech of King Alfred—of which our Dorset is the remnant— would have been the Court language of today.' His earlier poems are full of the love of rivers, as a random verse from one of them, entitled 'Vields by Watervalls', makes clear:

Here be softest airs ablowen,
Drough the boughs wi' zingen drushes,
Up above the streams, aflowen
Under willows, on by rushes.
Here below the bright zunned sky
The dew bespangled flow'rs do dry,
In woody-zided, stream-divided
Vields by flowen watervalls.

But the best known of Barnes' beautiful poems is perhaps the world-famous one of 'Linden Lea'.

Downstream from Fiddleford the Stour flows in a generally south-easterly direction past the villages of Manston, Hammoon, Child Okeford, Shillingstone and Durweston. Hammoon is a curious name, but easily explicable. It was the ham or home of the De Mohuns, a prominent Norman family who came over with the Conqueror and built themselves a manor here, so giving the place its identity. Shillingstone (or Shilling Okeford), lying beneath Shillingstone Hill, is a pleasant village and contains many delightful houses. It was formerly famous for its May revels and its maypole.

At this point, the Stour's valley becomes narrower, with steep chalk uplands such as Hod Hill, Hambledon Hill, and further afield Bulbarrow, (which at 902 feet is the highest point in Dorset), enclosing it on either side. Hod Hill, on the site of an Iron Age camp, is crowned by Roman fortifications; and Hambledon Hill was also fortified in pre-Roman times. Hambledon was the scene of a curious episode at the end of the Civil War in 1645, when the 'Clubmen' gathered there under their standards, announcing:

'If you plunder or take our cattle
Be sure we will bid you battle.'

Two thousand of these Dorset countrymen had banded themselves together there to resist plunder by either of the combatant sides in the Civil War; but they were no match for the disciplined Parliamentarian troops under Cromwell, who dispersed them without difficulty in a pitched encounter, cutting down some twelve or more of them before the others fled.

Eventually, about twelve miles downstream from Sturminster, the Stour reaches the handsome town of Blandford Forum, with its many fine Georgian buildings. Blandford is a country town of fair size, with a present population of around 4,500. It is of ancient foundation, but in 1731 it suffered a disastrous fire, which seems to have been no unusual fate for towns of that period. It is probable that many of the houses in country towns of that date had thatched roofs, which together with their wooden beams would have provided ready fuel for a conflagration. This particular fire destroyed most of the town, which was subsequently rebuilt in its present style, though modern development has largely increased its size. Its finest buildings are the Georgian Church of St. Peter and St. Paul, also an impressive Town Hall of similar period. Two miles upstream of Blandford, standing high above the south bank of the Stour, lies the large Bryanston House. This was formerly the home of the Portman family, but for over sixty five years now it has housed a well known public school.

Middle Stour near Spettisbury

Leaving Blandford, the Stour continues its south-easterly course past the villages of Charlton Marshall, Spetisbury, Shapwick, and Sturminster Marshall to Wimborne Minster. The countryside here has changed slightly in character, and is no longer quite like the lush pasturage of the Blackmoor Vale. The river valley with its water meadows is less wide, and the chalk uplands on either side border it more closely than upriver. So far as the river itself is concerned, however, there is little change except for a gradual increase in size.

Two miles north of Shapwick are the remains of the ancient Roman fortification of Badbury Rings, a prominent local landmark visible for many miles around. This was a foundation of considerable importance on the site of a pre-Roman fortification and trade route centre. 'Vindocladia' as it was known to the Romans, was where the roads from London to Exeter and Poole to Bath crossed. There are extensive circular earthworks here, and in their time the fortifications must have been elaborate. Mons Badonicus, or Badbury Rings as it came to be known, was most probably the site of the great battle of 'Mount Badon', won by Ambrosius or rather his general Arthur leading the British (or Welsh) forces against the invading Saxons in the late fifth or early sixth century (see p. 17). This crushing victory held up further Saxon influx for at least one generation, if not two.

Badbury Rings. Probable site of battle of Mount Badon won by Arthur over the Saxons

Some thirteen miles downstream of Blandford the Stour by-passes Wimborne Minster, another notable Dorset town with a modern population of about six thousand. Wimborne has a history reaching far back, beyond even the Middle Ages. Here is found one of the great churches of Dorset, the twin-towered Church of St. Cuthberga, a princess and daughter of the Saxon King Ine who founded Sherborne in the early years of the 8th century. Wimborne Minster, as it is known, reputedly built on the site of what was originally a pagan Roman temple, includes architecture of all styles, varying from Norman to late Gothic. There was also a nunnery here, founded by St. Cuthberga, its original Abbess, as early as around 713 AD, and the Minster followed its foundation. Wimborne was undoubtedly a place of importance in Saxon times, indicated by the fact that King Ethelred I, the elder brother of the great King Alfred, was buried here in 871 AD, after dying of wounds received in battle against the Danes. His younger brother, King Alfred, was almost certainly proclaimed King of Wessex here at Wimborne. Later, at the beginning of the 11th century, the original Wimborne Minster was sacked and destroyed by the Danes under Canute (before his conversion to Christianity). Subsequently Canute, having become King of all England and having embraced Christianity, encouraged the rebuilding of churches, as at Wareham and Wimborne, which in his younger days he had helped to destroy.

Since those early and troubled days Wimborne has led the peaceful existence of a modest sized country town, its fortunes in mediaeval times based largely on the wool trade; though more recently market gardening has played a prominent role. But sadly in the future Wimborne inevitably seems destined to lose its rural character, being already connected with the large urban areas of Poole and Bournemouth by almost continuous building, a feature of modern times.

Besides the Minster itself, Wimborne possesses several fine buildings, the most outstanding of which is undoubtedly Sir Michael Hanham's Dean's Court on its southern outskirts. The gardens and water meadows here border the Stour and its chief tributary, the Allen, which runs into the main river half a mile downstream. Dean's Court was originally the Deanery to the Wimborne Minster College of Canons, founded in 1100 AD. Traces of mediaeval structure are to be found in the basement of this house, and the story goes that there was once a secret passage from the Deanery to the Minster. In 1548, however, the College of Canons was closed, and the Deanery and its manors were granted to Sir John Hanham, the MP for Poole. The house and surrounding property have remained right up to the present date in the possession of the Hanham family. In 1725, the old house was enlarged and given a dark red brick facade; and again, in 1868, some rebuilding was done to the south side of the structure. There is a lovely garden, covering some 13 acres. Both building and grounds are remarkably handsome, and surprisingly secluded considering that they stand on the outskirts of the town.

Wimborne has other notable possessions of historical interest. One of these is described as an 'astronomical clock', housed in the Minster, and said to date from 1320 AD. Another is a chained library of 240 books, dated from 1686, while in the muniments room of the Minster is to be found an ancient Bible, together with Sir Walter Raleigh's *History of the World*, most of which he wrote while imprisoned in the Tower of London for thirteen years in the early 1600's.

Below Wimborne, for the fifteen miles of its lower reaches, except for the extensive grounds of Canford School, the Stour enters what is now virtually a built-up area before its junction with the Avon in its tidal reaches at Christchurch. On its right bank lie the widely spread suburbs of Bournemouth and Boscombe, and on its left the urban areas of Ferndown and Parley. Further downstream it passes between Southbourne and Christchurch. It is inevitable in these circumstances that the river loses much of its peaceful appeal. Close to Christchurch too are found the massive sewage works at Holdnenhurst, situated on the banks of the river. While these works do an admirable job in dealing with the huge amount of sewage emanating from so large an urban district, their effluent, which after treatment is discharged into the river, does not add to the Stour's attractions in this area.

The river is affected by high tides shortly before its junction with the Avon close to Christchurch Priory, which it skirts on its left bank, and it flows into the English Channel in combination with the Avon at Mudeford, a mile or so further downstream at the outlet from Christchurch Harbour.

Its tidal reaches at Christchurch provide a welcome anchorage for a great number of small pleasure craft.

Tidal Stour and Christchurch Priory

STOUR FISHING

Salmon

The record of the Stour as a salmon river is indeed depressing during these past fifteen years, as the record of rod catches given below makes clear. However, it must be remembered that a more unlikely looking salmon river is hard to imagine. Perhaps the wonder is that the Stour contrives to hold salmon at all.

The first essential for a salmon river, in order to be productive, is the possession of good spawning beds. Of these the main Stour with its solid, deep, and turgid flow, is badly deficient. Grimble in his *Salmon Rivers of England and Wales* (1904) talks of spawning beds in the main Stour up as far as Spetisbury, 10 miles above Wimborne. But nowadays it is unlikely that many of these are tenanted, and much of the spawning takes place either lower down the main river or else up a tributary, the little river Allen, which runs in at Wimborne. Salmon or grilse have on occasion been seen at spawning time in this latter river as far upstream as Stanbridge Mill, 8 miles above Wimborne, though few of them would ever have been successful in surmounting the various obstacles downstream such as the formidable hatches at Witchampton. What is more, in a recent case of pollution at least 12 adult salmon were found dead at Christmas time in the lower reaches of the Allen. This misfortune indicates without doubt that this small chalkstream with its mainly gravel bed does provide a limited amount of spawning ground; and with this and with such scattered beds as are available in the main river, or up the tributary Moors River, the Stour salmon have to make do. In addition the salmon fry, parr and smolts in their adolescence have to compete in the Allen with large numbers of brown trout and grayling, together with pike, and in the main Stour and Moors River with myriads of coarse fish of all types. It is surprising that any of them survive.

A major disaster for Stour salmon fishing was that some fifteen years ago large scale dredging operations had to be carried out in the neighbourhood of Throop Weir, a few miles upstream of Christ-church. The reason for this was the laudable one of flood prevention, coupled with land drainage; but unfortunately nearly all the good salmon lies at this point were either dredged out or artificially denuded of water. This salmon fishery at Throop, which formerly was by far the best on the whole river and contributed the bulk of the total catch, was thus ruined, and so far has never recovered. It was a sad disaster.

Elsewhere in the Stour it has always been difficult to pinpoint salmon lies. There is little ostensible reason why salmon should lie in any one place rather than another. Hatch pools, of which there are a fair number up and down this river, in the past have always offered the best chance, but nevertheless such salmon stock as there is in the Stour becomes widely scattered rather than being con-centrated in any definite pools. A thick weed growth adds to the difficulty of rod fishing.

In addition there is the hazard of pollution. Much of the Stour suffers a not inconsiderable amount of this. In the Blackmoor Vale area a good deal of farm sewage from time to time creeps into the river and its tributaries, and lower down between Wimborne and Christchurch inevitably there is some pollution from such a heavily urbanized area. The great sewage farm at Holdenhurst in addition discharges an effluent into the river, which although treated to a point where it is classed as harmless, is nevertheless by no means entirely pure. Amongst the tributaries, even the pure chalk stream Allen suffers severe pollution on occasions halfway down its course, and the little Crane or Moors River, joining the Stour at Hurn some two miles above Christchurch, is also polluted to a certain extent in its lower reaches. So, taking a general view, the position as regards pollution is none too happy. It has in fact been conjectured that as a result of this pollution some Stour fish having entered the estuary might prefer to ascend the unpolluted Avon rather than their own sullied parent river. While it is impossible to be certain about this, it might seem quite a possibility.

Turning to the nature and size of the runs of Stour salmon and grilse, the catch has become so attenuated in these last few years that it is difficult to estimate present trends. Presumably the size of fish is now, as it always has been, similar to that of the Avon. In past years this was large. In Grimble (1904) we read that the first fish ever to be taken by rod in the Stour was in 1873 and weighed 36 lb. From then on till about 1960 fish averaged around 20 lb in weight, and were almost without exception big springers, with plenty of 30 pounders amongst them. The record Stour fish, taken at Throop, weighed 48½ lb. But during the last 25 years the average size has gradually dwindled to its present level of under 10 lb, and the season's run has faded to its latest nadir when virtually no salmon are caught at all.

It is a sad story, and a nostalgic one. In the Badminton Magazine of 1895, for instance, the Countess of Malmesbury writing about the Stour says: 'Time sped away, and faintly, in the distance, I could hear the bell ringing for the servants' dinner at one o'clock . . . Now the one o'clock bell at Heron Court had come to be known as the salmon-bell, so surely did the fish rise at that time of day.' Doubtless Lady Malmesbury would have been disappointed with the show of fish in these present days!

This lady was undoubtedly a stalwart fisher, and she lived to a considerable age. In the same magazine she also described in detail the potentiality of the Stour as a salmon river in the 1880s and '90s, its rod catch developing from virtually nothing to a substantial total over a comparatively short space of time. She said that this development was helped by the disappearance of a big sandbank which had gone far towards blocking the Stour's flow close to its mouth. She recollected what she described as a 'Homeric combat' between herself and a large salmon which she hooked one April evening at Heron Court. Her lure was a fly tied by her ghillie, Dugald Cameron, and she played this fish for thirty-five minutes before Dugald got the gaff into it. It weighed 32 lb. Dugald unfortunately was later drowned through a hatch which he was drawing up suddenly collapsing, and allowing him to fall in and be swept by the downward rush into the main hatch pool. Lady Malmesbury described him thus: 'Like

A FIGHT FOR LIFE

so many Highlanders of that class he was a perfect gentleman in thought and manner, and a sportsman to the core.'

As regards netting, since Victorian times no netting has taken place in the Stour itself. But, as described in The Avon, netting has always taken place in the 'Run' at Mudeford, at the joint mouth of the Stour and Avon. A proportion of the salmon and grilse taken there, even if not a large one, must inevitably have been Stour fish. It is quite impossible however to calculate their numbers, mixed as they always have been with the Avon fish.

A summary of Stour salmon and grilse rod catches is given below. It shows clearly the rise and fall up to the present of the salmon fishing in this river.

Date	Average Yearly Rod Catch
1908 to 1917	29
1918 to 1927	21
1928 to 1937	16
1938 to 1947	19
1948 to 1957	46
1958 to 1967	58
1968 to 1970	19
1971 to 1973	9
1974 to 1976	1
1977 to 1979	3
1980	0
1981	2
1982	1
1983	1
1984	2
1985	0

The best catches were: 1955 — 103 fish.
1956 — 102 fish.
1965 — 102 fish.
The Salmon rod fishing season lasts from February 1st each year to September 30th.

Sea-trout

There are sea-trout to be found in the Stour, as in almost all south country rivers. But it cannot be claimed that the Stour is in any way a great sea-trout river. As in the case of salmon the mere existence of these fish could be regarded with a certain amount of surprise, (except that they enter almost every south coast river).

The average size of rod-caught sea-trout has varied little over the past forty years; it is around 2 lb, but much bigger fish are sometimes taken, occasionally reaching double figures in weight. The rod caught sea-trout average less in weight than those caught by net in the 'Run' at Mudeford, for the same reasons as in the Avon.

Most Stour sea-trout are caught on a bait, as little fly fishing is done in this river, and in addition they are seldom caught elsewhere than in the lower part of the river.

As to the spawning grounds, Stour sea-trout are not well endowed. Most of them have to make do with the main river itself, with all the attendant hazards to their progeny from every type of coarse fish, while some of them choose as an alternative the small Moors River tributary, which runs in at Hurn. This too is not ideal as a breeding ground owing to periodic pollution and the presence of coarse fish. Occasionally also some sea-trout spawn up the Allen.

A record of Stour sea-trout rod catches is as follows:

Date	Yearly Average of Sea-Trout caught
1951 to 1960	54
1961 to 1970	135
1971 to 1981	22
1982	33
1983	92
1984	17
1985	13

The sea-trout rod fishing season lasts from April 15th each year to October 31st.

157

Apart from this sea-trout fishing, there is no other trout fishing in the Stour worth mentioning. Brown trout do not thrive in this river, though in its main tributary, the Allen, they are abundant. There are also brown trout to be found in the Moors River, or Crane, in its upper reaches, almost as far upstream as Cranborne, though the Crane here is no more than a small brook. Occasional brown trout are also caught in the Stour's headwaters, though in no number.

Coarse Fishing

Stour coarse fishing in recent times presents a very different picture to that of the Avon. It was always good, but in the past fifteen or so years, particularly in the river's lowest reaches, it has consistently improved. The five miles of water upstream from Christchurch have lately provided excellent fishing, better perhaps than ever before. All the main species of coarse fish are to be found here in numbers, barbel, roach, dace, chub, pike, and to a lesser extent carp, tench and perch.

Although the best fishing is to be found low down the river, from Throop Mill downstream, the whole of the rest of the Stour, upstream past Sturminster Newton, even as far as Gillingham, where the river has become very small, holds a good stock of coarse fish, and except in one area (see below) has been recently showing improvement. It is true there is a certain amount of pollution from farm or urban sewage in the West Parley to Christchurch area; but this is seldom enough to do substantial harm to the coarse fish, which can stand up to a modest degree of it better than can game fish. The Wessex Water Authority is in any case taking great trouble to keep this pollution under strict control, and where possible to eliminate it.

There has however been a sad disaster further upstream this past year (1985) when during September there was a serious pollution in the Marnhull—Sturminster Newton area. This was attributed to farm sewage, and its effects were all the more serious as the river flow was at low summer level at the time. Roach were the main sufferers, some 3,200 being killed. Other casualties were 300 pike, 260 chub, and 120 perch, as well as smaller numbers of dace, carp, tench, and bream. It will be some time, unfortunately, before the ill-effects of this débacle will cease to be felt in the area affected, although the Wessex Water Authority has restocked on a generous scale. Fortunately on this occasion no harm was done downstream of Fiddleford, but periodic pollution from farm sewage in the Blackmoor Vale area is always a hazard.

Turning back to the lower Stour fishing, the biggest improvement has taken place on the Hurn Estate water, from Throop Mill downstream, which belongs to Lord FitzHarris, and after Water Authority dredging operations caused the main stream to bypass the Throop Mill Pool and eliminated the salmon lies in that area. With the salmon fishing at a discount, extra attention has been given by Lord Fitz-Harris to the improvement of the coarse fishing. Selective weed cutting and good general management have produced well deserved results; and there is no finer coarse fishing to be found in the whole country than here.

Specimen fish from the lower Stour include the following: barbel 12 lb, carp 15 lb, roach $2\frac{1}{2}$ lb. Chub in the past have been recorded up to 6 lb, but only this year (1986) a magnificent fish of 7 lb 1 oz has been reported as being taken from the Throop water on bread-flake fished on a size 12 hook to $1\frac{1}{2}$ lb B.S. nylon.

Coarse fishing in the middle reaches of the river near Wimborne Minster is also highly rated; while further upstream in the Blandford and Fiddleford area the Stour again has always been noted for excellent fishing. It is generally regarded as a 'winter river', when the weed has died down and the higher river flows help towards good results.

While there are no barbel or grayling in the middle or upper reaches, and only a few trout in the headwaters, fish of other species are plentiful. Specimen roach abound, sometimes reaching 3 lb in weight, and chub up to $5\frac{1}{4}$ lb are also present in numbers, providing good sport (the largest in fact reached 7 lb $14\frac{1}{2}$ oz). They can sometimes be caught on a fly, particularly in hatch pools. Good flies for this purpose include Wickham's Fancy, Coachman, Alder, Zulu, Blue

Sturminster Mill

Bottle, and Palmers (red and black), all fished dry. Chub are not fastidious in their choice of fly. They are in addition undoubtedly predatory at times, and will on occasion take salmon anglers' golden sprats or other spun baits. Bream, a recent introduction, are flourishing, and occasionally reach 8 lb. Pike are also plentiful, with outsized specimens of up to 20 lb. Tench can be caught up to 6 lb, and perch up to 3 lb or over. Favourable conditions also hold good further upstream above Sturminster—but sadly of course the resultant effects of the large scale pollution from Marnhull downwards, mentioned above, have still to be felt. The outcome cannot fail, temporarily, to be disadvantageous in that six mile stretch of water.

Methods of fishing in the Stour are the normal ones, either float trotting or ledgering (often with a swim feeder) so far as shoal fish are concerned.

There are a number of mills and weirs on the upper Stour, the

PLATE 10

Fiddleford Mill, river Stour

A painting by Paul Stewart

PLATE 11

The river Allen at Wimborne St. Giles

The Allen at Brockington

most noted being at Highbridge (West Stour), Stour Provost, Cuttmill (Hinton St. Mary), Sturminster, Fiddleford, Durweston, Bryanston, and Blandford.

Hatch pools or weir pools are almost always a gathering place for fish of all sorts, and help greatly in providing good fishing. Sturminster mill pool and Fiddleford mill pool are both outstanding in this respect.

Such pools below Blandford and downstream as far as Throop Mill are fewer in number, but still exist at intervals and are of similar benefit to anglers.

In conclusion it could fairly be said that the Stour is one of the best coarse fishing rivers in the whole country—perhaps not quite up to the exceptional standard of its sister river the Avon; but nevertheless, with little to choose between them, it provides fishing of an outstanding quality.

Fiddleford Mill

Witchampton Bridge, river Allen

A drawing by Paul Stewart

THE ALLEN
AND ITS FISHING

The main tributary of the Stour is a lovely pure chalk stream, of some 13 miles length—the Allen. The ancient name for for it appears to have been the 'Win', as Wimborne Minster at its junction with the Stour is designated 'Winborne' in the Domesday Book (1086), and is obviously named after its river. Hutchins in his 'History of Dorset' (1774) says that in Roman times the river was most probably known as the 'Vind' or 'Vindo', recast in Saxon times as the 'Win'.

More than a thousand years later, when he wrote his 'History', Hutchins still describes Wimborne Minster as 'Winbourn' Minster. He also refers to 'Winborne St. Giles', 'Winborne All Saints', and 'Upwinborn-Monkton', all villages on the course of this river; but to him this latter has become the 'Allen'. Presumably this name was established sometime in the early Middle Ages.

Like the Ebble and other chalk streams, the Allen in its uppermost reaches is a winter bourne. Its permanent summer source is in springs halfway between Wimborne St. Giles and Monkton, ten miles north of Wimborne Minster, but with a high water table in late winter or early spring its headwaters often break from the chalk subsoil two further miles upstream close to the Salisbury–Blandford turnpike road. It then flows through the village of Monkton, then Wimborne St. Giles and past St. Giles House (where as a matter of interest Handel, Kapelle-meister to King George II, once paid a visit and composed). The main part of this house has a Tudor foundation, as anyone who inspects its basement can easily perceive. It was probably built on the site of an earlier house of the Norman or Plantagenet era. In the 17th and 18th centuries it was extended, and had wide-spread gardens and pleasure grounds. The stables, separated from the house, are buildings dating from mediaeval times, older than the house itself. Subsequent to the Norman conquest Wimborne St. Giles came into the possession of the Malmayne family, who also owned property in Hampshire, then of the Plecys, and Hamelyns, and since the late 1400s of the Ashleys, who hailed from near Bradford on Avon, all linked through a series of marriages with heiresses.

Wimborne St. Giles Georgian Church and early 17th century almshouses

One of the Allen's branches flows through an artificial lake here, to rejoin the main river a short distance downstream. Immediately below this the Allen by-passes the lost villages of Knowlton and Brockington. Knowlton was a royal manor at the time of Domesday Book, and in the Middle Ages was a substantial village along the left bank of the Allen, with an annual fair of its own, also its own mill. Knowlton church, though a ruin, still stands on neighbouring high ground, and is situated in the middle of a prehistoric circular earthwork. This church forms a noted local landmark, and dates from the 12th century, though enlarged in the 15th century, which suggests a then local population of considerable size. It was not used after the mid-seventeenth century when the village of Knowlton disappeared, perhaps owing to an outbreak of plague.

Opposite Knowlton, on the right bank of the Allen, lay another village known as Brockington, on the site of which only a farmhouse and one or two cottages still remain. This village also, in mediaeval times, was quite sizeable, and appears to have covered some ten acres, being separated from Knowlton only by the river. Brockington village too disappeared about the same time as Knowlton, though a walled paddock still remains which housed one of the first three Arab stallions introduced into this country (in the mid-seventeenth century). In present days there is a trout farm here.

Below Brockington the Allen pursues its course through water meadows for a further three miles as far as Crichel and Witchampton. There are mills and hatches en route at the Bone Mill, Stanbridge Mill, Loverley, and Didlington, but all these mills are now out of commission with the hatches (except at Stanbridge Mill) drawn or disintegrated. Near Stanbridge Mill there is a bore-hole which abstracts anything up to five million gallons of water daily from underground sources throughout the year for the benefit of the Poole and Bournemouth water supply and that of the district. Whether this is a wise method of meeting ever-increasing demands for water is open to argument. The normal flow of the Allen, although it rises to as high as seventy million gallons daily, or more, during the late winter or spring, is apt to sink to its usual low water volume of five million gallons daily in the dry months of July, August and September. It would seem therefore that in this case mankind is trying artificially to contrive the discharge of the equivalent of two summer streams from sources in the chalk which by nature are only designed to produce a single one. This in the long run is unlikely to be a satisfactory solution.

In spite of this drain on its resources, and except for a period in late summer and autumn, the Allen as yet still has adequate flow to retain its natural character and to provide good dry fly fishing, though there is no room for any increased water abstraction in the future.

Two miles below Stanbridge this river reaches the big mill at Witchampton, mentioned in Domesday Book as a grain mill, but for the last three hundred years producing paper. The fall at the mill hatches here is a high one, and makes the ascent for any fish extremely difficult. Nevertheless, salmon moving up from the Stour to Allen spawning grounds have occasionally been known to surmount it.

At Witchampton there is a red brick bridge of long standing date across the river, which as in the case of a number of other bridges in Dorset (see p. 142) carries the notice as shown, inscribed on an iron plate bolted to its parapet:

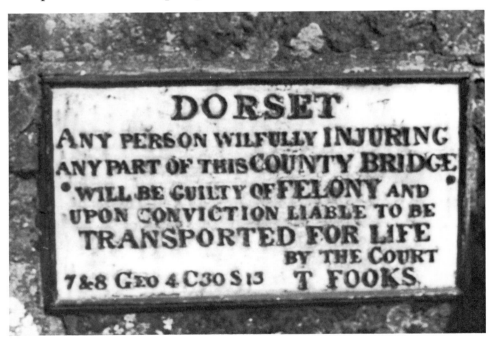

'A free passage to Australia?' as someone in these modern days drily commented!

Below Witchampton, with its picturesque bridge, the Allen for a mile or so is owned by Crichel on the right bank and Gaunts on the left, until further downstream Gaunts takes over both banks for one and a half more miles. Below this lies the High Hall water and the town water of Wimborne Minster, while for its final half mile before entering the Stour, the Allen flows through Sir Michael Hanham's property at Dean's Court, on the southern outskirts of Wimborne.

Over most of its length above Wimborne the Allen provides good dry fly fishing. In former days, before it was artificially stocked, there was a fair head of wild trout, particularly at Gaunts and Wimborne St. Giles; but fishing then was not so intensive as it is now. Wild trout in those days averaged around $\frac{1}{2}$ to $\frac{3}{4}$ lb in weight, and any fish of over one pound was a large one. Now much more fishing takes place on all the Allen beats, such as Wimborne St. Giles, Crichel, Gaunts and High Hall, so that owners or tenants have had to fall back on stocking to furnish the required catch. A fair sized bag is now made on all these waters, and nothing under $\frac{3}{4}$ lb is killed. The bags on the St. Giles fishery, for instance, during recent years run as follows:

1980–297	1983–385
1981–310	1984–557
1982–315	1985–650

with an average weight of $1\frac{1}{2}$ lb. This water is kept plentifully stocked.

The fly hatch of the Allen has always been somewhat sparse, and perhaps not improved by any insecticide sprayed on nearby fields. However, it is adequate, and a Pheasant Tail, highly floated, is often successful. May fly normally appear towards the end of May, though not in large quantities. Perhaps this is just as well from the fishing point of view.

Odd salmon arrive in the Allen at spawning time, as already mentioned, but not during the fishing season. There was a bad case of pollution at Christmas 1983 on the lower half of the river below

Witchampton, when at least twelve salmon were found dead, as well as a large number of trout and other fish. Other salmon may perhaps have survived. It appears that many of the salmon which enter the Stour at Christchurch spawn in the lower reaches of the Allen, as well as some up the little Moors River which runs into the Stour lower down near Hurn.

Few redds are now to be found in the Stour itself, which in any case is to some extent polluted from farm sewage in the Blackmoor Vale and from urban sewage lower down. The Allen only occasionally appears to harbour spawning sea-trout, though a number of these fish do spawn up the Moors River, which has a higher acid content, (the Allen water being pronouncedly alkaline.)

Grayling are to be found in the Allen low down near Wimborne,

The Allen
near High Hall

Dry fly water at Stanbridge Mill, river Allen

also a few coarse fish such as dace and roach occur here, also in the Crichel water.

Pike from Stanbridge Mill downstream are always a hazard, though above this point they are rare. Annual electric fishing from Stanbridge Mill down has helped, however, to keep their numbers under control. Coarse fish of all sorts abound in the Stour, and there is little to stop them edging their way upriver into the Allen.

As to other unwanted denizens of this lovely chalk stream and its banks, herons are perhaps the worst. There used to be a heronry at Crichel which formerly was allowed to flourish, but it may have disappeared now. Herons are a permanent menace to trout on such small streams as the Allen, particularly at spawning time. They are not rare birds, and are common almost everywhere on south-country rivers. The late Major T. T. Phelps, an expert angler and Chairman for many years of the Test and Itchen Fishing Association, made these succinct remarks about herons in his wellknown book *Fishing Dreams*: 'In the deeper, heavier and more sluggish reaches of most trout streams in southern England, Public Enemy No. 1 is the pike, and in the upper and shallower, the heron. Both are deadly and demand constant vigilance.'

Kingfishers are sometimes to be seen on the Allen, to everyone's delight. Otters used to inhabit its banks in years long past, but alas! have vanished now. They never did any harm, and were charming visitors or residents.

Over its course the Allen has two sizeable tributaries, the Gussage Brook which runs in above Stanbridge Mill, and the Crichel Brook which feeds Crichel lake and escapes through the outflow to join the main river above Witchampton. Both these brooks are winter bournes in their headwaters, and are at no time of any great size; nevertheless, they help to maintain the Allen's flow, a vital need in these days of water abstraction, and provide spawning grounds for trout in their lowest reaches.

The Allen is a lovely stream. While very pleasant in character and holding a good head of fish, it must be admitted that parts of its course are somewhat neglected, and rushes and weed are too often left to choke it during summer. Also hatches have been drawn or allowed to disintegrate in a number of places, which lowers the water level and is apt sometimes to make the stream too thin and fast. It also suffers as a result of the water abstraction mentioned above, and from periodic pollution in its lower half. The River Allen Association and the various riparian owners do their best to struggle with these problems, with some measure of success; and it is to be hoped such success will continue in the future.

THE PIDDLE
AND ITS FISHING

The Piddle (or Trent) is a small river, nevertheless one of note, being a pure chalk stream of around twenty-two miles in length, and a handsome enhancement to the natural beauty of the Dorset countryside. The name 'Piddle' is without doubt of Saxon origin, and as recounted in Hutchins *History of Dorset* (1774) it is quoted as 'Pidele' in the Domesday Book (1086).

It has the distinction of harbouring three types of indigenous game fish, salmon, sea-trout and brown trout, all in fair numbers, which is unusual for so small a river. It also holds some rainbow trout of recent introduction.

The Piddle rises near Alton Pancras, a village eight miles due north of Dorchester, though in summer tends not to emerge above ground till the neighbouring village of Piddletrenthide, a further three miles downstream. Its valley is a narrow one up here, with downland on either side. Piddletrenthide boasts a lovely fifteenth century church. About two miles further down the river, which runs southwards, is Piddlehinton, another small but attractive village. Here the Piddle turns south-eastwards, and its valley starts to open out. A further three miles, passing en route the Blue Vinny Inn, a reminder of Dorset's local cheese industry, takes it to Puddletown, a larger village on the main road from Blandford to Dorchester, with a population of about 1,000. A mile east of Puddletown on the banks of the Piddle lies the beautiful mediaeval manor of Athelhampton, dating from 1483, which contains fine furniture, a minstrels' gallery, and has an attractive garden close by the river. Tolpuddle is the next village on the Piddle's course, then Affpuddle, Bryantspuddle, and Throop. About three miles downstream of Throop the Piddle passes close to the well known Hyde House, built in the eighteenth century and formerly the home of the Radclyffe family. Hyde House has a useful stretch of river, and is now a country club. Finally after a further

Athelhampton manor house

four miles the river arrives at its tidal reaches, skirting on its right bank the high ground on which Wareham is situated. It enters Poole Harbour one and a half miles further downstream at Swineham Point, having completed a total course of about twenty-two miles. Its mouth is separate from that of the Frome, and about half a mile from it, although both rivers empty into the same branch of the Harbour.

Its whole catchment area amounts to around 79 square miles. It is thus by no means a big river, but is one of peculiar charm, flowing through a delightful valley bordered by downland or farmland, and in its lower reaches heathland and occasionally woodland. Like all chalk rivers it is liberally endowed with water meadows on either bank.

The Piddle has two main tributaries, both pure chalk streams and both joining it from the north. The first is the Devil's Brook, which rises near Bingham's Melcombe, south of Bulbarrow, and runs due south past Dewlish until after about five miles it joins the main river at Athelhampton, between Puddletown and Tolpuddle. The second is the Milborne Brook or Bere Stream, flowing from Milton Abbas via Milborne St. Andrew and Bere Regis to unite with the Piddle five miles upstream from Wareham. Neither of these tributaries is of any great size, the latter being slightly the larger, but together they bring a valuable increase to the Piddle's flow.

Tolpuddle, mentioned above, was the scene in 1833 of the well-known episode involving the 'Tolpuddle Martyrs', six farm labourers of the neighbourhood, who had combined to demand higher wages. These men were arrested and convicted at Dorchester Crown Court under an Act of 1797, which made it a felony, punishable by up to seven years transportation, 'to adminster an oath binding a person to belong to any association to disturb the publick peace', 'to obey the orders of any committee not lawfully constituted', and 'not to reveal an illegal oath'. They were sentenced to seven years transportation to Australia's penal settlements. There is no place here to discuss in detail the rights and wrongs of this sentence. By modern standards it was, of course, unjust; and even too severe by the standards of the times, as it caused a nationwide public protest. But it should be appreciated the French Revolution from 1789 onwards, with all its horrors and subsequent war-making, at this time was well within living memory, the 1820's had seen much unrest amongst the agricultural labouring community of Dorset with rick and barn burning and rioting, and consequently there was considerable public uneasiness. However, all six 'martyrs' received a free pardon after two years from Lord John Russell, the Home Secretary, and all of them were back in Britain shortly afterwards. Five of them formed a group and emigrated to Ontario in Canada, where they seem to have settled down well, one of them eventually becoming Mayor of East London. So they did not suffer too badly after all. (The sixth 'martyr' resumed life in Tolpuddle.) This sequel has been largely overlooked in more recent times.

In Hutchins' *History of Dorset* (1774), the prefix or suffix 'Piddle' is everywhere used in local names now employing 'Puddle'; e.g.

Hutchins writes of 'Piddletown', 'Tolpiddle', 'Turner's Piddle', 'Aff Piddle', and so on. There is no doubt that this was the original form of nomenclature.

When 'Puddle' was substituted in such names is not certain, but it was sometime in the earlier half of the 19th century. The story goes that this was done to avoid giving any possible grounds of offence to Queen Victoria, when she was visiting the neighbourhood, which may or may not be true!

Tolpuddle. The sycamore tree where the 'martyrs' met

Salmon Fishing

The Piddle, it might be thought, owing to its character and small size, would be an unlikely stream to hold salmon and grilse. But this is not the case. These fish ascend it every year from Poole Harbour, as the following record of its salmon and grilse rod catches show:

1970 –	7	1978 –	9
1971 –	24	1979 –	15
1972 –	69	1980 –	40
1973 –	26	1981 –	27
1974 –	24	1982 –	10
1975 –	24	1983 –	24
1976 –	7	1984 –	16
1977 –	25	1985 –	19

The average weight of these fish is similar to that of the Frome fish, i.e. around 10 lb in present times, though as in the Frome it used to be much higher. Big fish are still occasionally caught; one of 34 lb was taken in the spring of 1985; in such a small river it must have seemed a veritable porpoise. The record Piddle salmon was even larger. It was caught by the late Mr. Wood-Homer one mile upstream from Wareham, and weighed 40 lb. This was in 1930.

The fishing season for salmon in this river lasts from March 1st till September 30th each year, and for sea-trout from April 15th till October 31st.

Although the Piddle itself is not now netted, a certain number of its salmon must, like Frome fish, fall to the net in Poole Harbour. When caught by net there it would be impossible to distinguish them from Frome fish and so to assess their number; but this is unlikely to be large.

Most of the salmon and grilse which enter the Piddle remain in the Wareham area until the autumn, and that is where they are usually caught by rod. A few push on to two or three miles above Wareham, but it is not until October as a rule, after the end of the fishing season, that there is a general upward movement of fish, spreading themselves over the eight mile stretch as far as Tolpuddle. This is the area where almost all spawning takes place, most of it within five miles of Wareham.

So Piddle salmon fishing is limited, both in extent and catch, but it can hardly be expected otherwise in a river of such small size. Indeed, this river is too narrow for the salmon to give a proper account of itself when hooked, the river bed being seldom of more than eight yards width. Casting in such a small river also becomes very cramped; in fact, there is sometimes little need to cast at all where the stream runs deep under the near bank. Any discriminating salmon fisherman would undoubtedly prefer for choice a much wider and deeper stream with a stronger current.

Sea-trout fishing

As well as salmon, the Piddle has a modest run of sea-trout. During the fishing season these fish mostly remain, like the salmon, well downstream in the Wareham area. The following is a record of sea-trout rod catches in recent years:

1970 –	42	1978 –	41
1971 –	31	1979 –	139
1972 –	27	1980 –	89
1973 –	10	1981 –	78
1974 –	16	1982 –	73
1975 –	18	1983 –	23
1976 –	23	1984 –	88
1977 –	20	1985 –	32

Most of these sea-trout are caught on bait in tidal water. Their average weight is, as in the Frome, around 2 lb, but much bigger fish sometimes appear. In addition to the rod catches, a certain number of Piddle sea-trout must also be caught by net in Poole Harbour. But their number again would be impossible to assess as distinct from the Frome fish. As in the Frome the rod caught sea-trout average less in weight than those caught by net in Poole Harbour, and for the same reasons.

An outstanding capture was made on September 25th, 1979, by Lt. Commander D. Crampton-Thomas who, fishing with an eight foot rod, successfully landed a huge sea-trout of 14 lb. This fish took an orange bodied nymph, size 10, fished on nylon mono-filament of $3\frac{3}{4}$ lb breaking strain. The struggle lasted for an hour, and this monster was only landed with great difficulty, as the trout landing net

PLATE 12

The Piddle near Throop

The Frome at Bindon—Kelt Alley, a good lie for salmon

PLATE 13

Aylmer Tryon at Bindon Mill

Wool Bridge, river Frome

which was available, being much too small in size, was of little use. However, somehow all was brought to a successful conclusion. This surely was the achievement of a lifetime, especially considering the light tackle involved; no angler could fail to be proud of it.

The spawning grounds of sea-trout in the Piddle are mainly in the lower and middle reaches, in the same area in fact as those of the salmon. As in other south-country rivers, these fish seldom penetrate far upstream.

In summary, therefore, although the Piddle could by no means be classed as an outstanding sea-trout river compared with many further to the West or North, nevertheless in this capacity it has its merits, and should by no means be overlooked.

Brown Trout Fishing

It is however for its brown trout fishing with the dry-fly that the Piddle is chiefly renowned. Mr. H. Wood-Homer of Bardolf Manor, near Puddletown, an expert all-round fisherman, has kindly provided much interesting information about it for this book.

Although good fishing is to be found on most parts of the Piddle, the middle reaches between Briantspuddle and Hyde are perhaps the best. There is a good fly hatch generally, particularly of mayfly, but also of olives, pale wateries, sedges, and B.W.O. There is excellent spawning ground in the Piddle, and wild trout are prolific. It follows that there is seldom any need for stocking. (Little in fact is done, except in parts of the middle and lower reaches where angling pressure is more intense and where wild fish are not plentiful enough to produce the required bags.) Above Affpuddle, for instance, keepable wild fish average 1 lb in weight, a good size not often attained elsewhere. Mr. Wood-Homer's biggest on the Piddle weighed 3 lb 10 ounces. During the mayfly time it is often possible for a skilled performer to take three brace of fish in a day each of 1 lb or over, and specimen fish of up to 4 lb have been caught in the past. It is emphasized again that these are mainly wild fish and not stew-reared.

The weed growth is good and plentiful; and owners or tenants have to do their own weed cutting, though the Water Authority sometimes cuts weed on the lower part of the river by arrangement with the owners there.

Coarse fish are not a problem. Pike occur only below Tolpuddle, and there are no grayling.

Water abstraction from the Piddle catchment area is only in minor amounts, though it does give cause for some anxiety. Up to one million gallons per day are taken from close to Alton Pancras, and a similar amount from near Dewlish. Near Briantspuddle too there is

River Piddle near Hyde. Good dry fly water

further abstraction. The flow of the Piddle is thereby lessened, to the concern of the riparian owners.

There is only one small fish farm in the Piddle valley, but no large-scale enterprise of this kind, so the Piddle is fortunate to be free from consequent risk of disease spreading into its waters.

Besides the Piddle itself, its main tributary the Devil's Brook also provides good fishing, although it is small. Some of its pools are artificially aided by bank revetting which confines and deepens the water, so that fish like to gather in them. Big fish are sometimes to be found in these, out of all proportion to the small size of the brook.

Taking an all round view, the Piddle is a delightful river, and it would be hard to find better dry fly fishing anywhere else in the Wessex area.

The Blue Vinny Inn at Puddletown. A reminder of Dorset's local cheese industry

River Frome at Bindon. In its lower reaches the river seems to twist and turn to an amazing degree

THE FROME

The Frome is entirely a Dorset river from source to mouth. Its name is said to be of Celtic derivation, but if so was passed on through the Saxon and Norman eras, as it appears in its present form in the Domesday Book of 1086.

It is not to be confused with the Somerset river of the same name, which runs through the town of Frome and into the Bristol Avon; but rising a mile west of Evershot in west Dorset it has a mainly eastward course of about thirty-five miles before running into Poole Harbour, one mile and a half below Wareham.

The Frome rises in rolling chalkland country with steep valleys, the sides of which are chalk with underlying beds of greensand. In the lower half of its course it runs over a sand and clay bed, adequately supplied with gravel. It has various tributaries in its higher reaches; the uppermost of these is the Hooke stream from the west, which runs in at Maiden Newton, followed by the Sydling Brook and the Cerne from the north. Below Dorchester, which lies fourteen miles downstream from its source, the Frome is joined by several small tributaries from the south, the largest of these being the Tadnol Brook and the Win. It is fair to call the Frome a chalk river, since its headwaters and those of its tributaries originate mainly from chalk spring sources; and certainly for the upper half of its course it has all the characteristics of a chalk stream. Its catchment area is one of approximately one hundred and ninety square miles. Its rate of flow in high water might fairly be estimated at an average of four knots, or in low water at half that speed, so it cannot be called a fast-running river and its current is about comparable with that of the Avon.

The Frome's admirable chalk stream character persists via Maiden Newton and Dorchester at least as far as West Stafford. It has for the most part a clear gravel bottom, good weed growth, lush water meadows, and a good stock of wild brown trout. It also has clear unpolluted water, a reasonable rate of flow, and a copious hatch of fly. The peaceful unspoilt Dorset countryside enhances the view on either bank. What more could any discerning country lover or dry fly fisherman desire?

Dorchester marks the end of the Frome's upper reaches. This county town of Dorset has a long history of considerable interest. It presumably had a pre-Roman British origin, but it first came into prominence as the Roman town of Durnovaria, founded about 70 AD after the Roman subjugation of this part of the country. It certainly became a prosperous town. The many tessellated pavements and the hoard of 22,000 coins recently unearthed there are evidence of this. Also it was in due course of considerable size, since the amphitheatre at Maumbury Rings, outside the town's south wall, has been judged capable of holding ten thousand people (Dorchester's modern population numbering about 15,000). Besides this, it was an important road junction, where the road south from Bath via Ilchester met the London–Exeter road.

In Anglo-Saxon England, Dorchester, as the county town of Dorset, survived an age of violence owing to the Danish invasions, interspersed with periods of tranquillity in which piety, learning and art all played their part.

Sheep and the wool and cloth trade were always economic factors of the highest importance to country towns such as this one, and this was the case right on into mediaeval times and thereafter. The sheep and their wool were the basic foundation of Dorchester's prosperity. In Domesday Book (1086) it is recorded that the largest Dorset manors held as many as 1,000 to 1,600 sheep. No doubt these numbers were increased in later times; in fact Defoe, writing in 1724 after a tour of Dorset, records the information that 600,000 sheep were grazing within six miles of the centre of Dorchester at that period.

Under Norman rule and during the Middle Ages, Dorchester continued a comparatively peaceful existence, untouched by the many wars of the period. A great catastrophe subsequently occurred in King James I's time, when in 1613 the town was devastated by both plague and fire, the latter destroying 300 houses. Episodes of this kind bring home to one the hazards and uncertainty of life in those days, medical knowledge being primitive, and fire fighting methods being presumably limited to bucket and chain—hopeless to compete with a well-established conflagration of timbered and thatched buildings. So often one reads of other devastating fires of this type, for example at Wareham, Blandford Forum, and above all in London.

During the earlier part of King Charles I's reign in the 17th century it became apparent that Dorchester had decided Puritan leanings. At any rate its M.P. in 1629 was the notorious Puritan Denzil Holles, who, when the Speaker of the House of Commons tried to leave the Chair and refused to read resolutions condemning firstly the collection of customs duties without Parliament's consent and secondly Laud's innovations in religion, together with another M.P. forcibly held the Speaker down in his chair whilst the resolutions were passed. 'You shall sit here till *we* please to rise', declared Holles. With the dissolution of Parliament Holles was imprisoned in the Tower of London, though he was subsequently released. Afterwards in 1642 Holles was one of the five notable members of Parliament whom King Charles I attempted to arrest, entering the House of Commons with a troop of swordsmen for that purpose, only to find that 'the birds were flown'. It was this action that went far towards precipitating the Civil War, and later we find Denzil Holles commanding a regiment both at Edgehill and in subsequent battles.

It followed that during the Civil War, which started that same year, Dorchester appears not unexpectedly to have been firmly Parliamentarian in sympathy. It paid a sad price for this, as in 1643 it was sacked by Prince Maurice's Royalist troops with all the horror that that entailed. It was, however, recaptured for Parliament in 1644 by the Earl of Essex.

Monmouth's rebellion in 1685 was another unfortunate episode in Dorchester's story. The recruiting of a substantial number of Dorset men for Monmouth's army (he landed at Lyme Regis) resulted, after his defeat at Sedgemoor, in Judge Jefferies' 'Bloody Assizes' at Dorchester. Of the 300 men there tried, 74 were executed, and 175 transported to the West Indies. This seems perhaps a modest 'justice' compared with what was sometimes perpetrated by our Norman and Plantagenet Kings or, for that matter, by the Waffen-S.S. in German occupied countries during the last war. Nevertheless, it left a long-lasting feeling of shock in Dorset, and antagonism to the rule of King James II and to the Jacobite cause.

Since that time Dorchester's existence has been a comparatively undisturbed one, except for the unrest during the 1820s and 1830s, owing to the combination of low agricultural wages, a disastrous harvest in 1829, and the uneasiness caused by the introduction of such labour-saving devices as threshing machines.

The Crimean War, in 1854, gave an impetus to agriculture around Dorchester, as elsewhere, after what seems to be the normal pattern of this country's large scale wars in this present age.

The opening of the first Dorset railway line took place in 1847. It ran from Southampton via Ringwood, Wimborne and Poole to Wareham and Dorchester, and subsequently connected with the line that ran on to Weymouth. It could be looked upon as ushering Dorchester into the modern age. From Wareham to Dorchester this railway still runs parallel with the Frome, and close by its course at frequent intervals, as many fishermen know.

The great Dorset writer, Thomas Hardy, lived in the neighbourhood of Dorchester for most of his life. Hardy was born at Higher Bockhampton, two miles from Dorchester. Towns which appear in his novels are Dorchester ('Casterbridge'), Weymouth ('Budmouth'), Bere Regis ('Kingsbere') and Puddletown ('Weatherbury'). His birthplace now belongs to the National Trust. Hardy was born in 1840 and lived till 1928. In 1910, when he was 70, he received the Order of Merit and the Freedom of Dorchester. His works concerned mainly the county of Dorset, but also from time to time covered the other counties of Wessex. He was a master of literature, and was buried in Westminster Abbey, though his heart was interred separately in the churchyard at Stinsford, just outside Dorchester, amid the countryside which he loved so dearly.

Near Bockhampton too is the Hardy Memorial, not to Thomas the author, but to Admiral Sir Thomas Hardy, Nelson's Flag Captain at

Higher Bockhampton—river Frome. Thomas Hardy's Cottage

the Battle of Trafalgar in 1805, another distinguished son of Dorset, who was born at Kingston Russell House between Dorchester and Bridport in 1769. He lived to become First Sea Lord in 1830, and Vice-Admiral in 1837, before his death in 1839.

Another famous local character of more recent date was Lawrence of Arabia, whose name is still revered in the Arab world as well as in his native country. The cottage to which he retired after the Great War is close to Moreton, and halfway between the Frome and the Piddle. It was here that he prepared the text of his *Seven Pillars of Wisdom*, and near Wool that he suffered his tragic and fatal motor-bike accident in 1935.

Returning to the Frome, below Dorchester it has achieved the status of a fair-sized river, reinforced by the Sydling Brook and the Cerne. Its course now lies via West Stafford, Woodsford, Moreton and Wool, eventually to Wareham. It passes the Atomic Energy

Authority's establishment near Winfrith just upstream of Wool, and the large military base of Bovington Camp. Near East Stoke is installed an extensive branch of the Freshwater Biological Association, which does much good research work about river and still-water biology of every description.

At East Stoke hatch the F.B.A. has installed and maintains a photographic and electrical fish counter, which records the passage of every sizeable fish passing upstream at this point. Although it may be difficult to achieve total accuracy as regards the numbers of salmon and grilse passing through this counter, as opposed to sea-trout, brown trout, pike, eels, mullet, and other fish, at least this counter must make clear the general trend of salmon movements upstream, both as regards comparative yearly numbers and the time of year when the ascent is made. For this reason alone its reading is of considerable interest.

East Stoke hatch, fish counter in middle

A curious feature of the course of the Frome in this area of its lower reaches is its extraordinarily serpentine character. It seems to twist and turn to an amazing degree, more so than any other river of the neighbourhood. In more than one place, two fishermen can be casting back to back within twenty five yards of each other, yet one be fishing three hundred yards or more downstream of the other. This may be hard to believe; nevertheless, it is an indisputable fact.

More than one link with the past is found on this stretch of the river, quite apart from the ancient townships of Dorchester and Wareham. For instance, the remains of the great Cistercian Abbey of Bindon, 'dissolved' by King Henry VIII, are well worth inspection. The buildings here, in their heyday early in the 16th century, must have approached in size those of an Oxford or Cambridge college. Little is left of them now; but the lay-out can clearly be traced, even down to the feeder streams and positioning of the fish stews, which housed the fare for fast days. What a disaster it must have been, not only for the monks but for all the neighbouring countryside, when great ancient and beneficent establishments such as this were brutally sequestered by the King's Commissioners, and allowed to fall into ruin.

Other relics of the past are many, such as the little church at East Stoke, dating from 1828 though its foundations are much older, and the lovely manor house with its bridge over the river at Wool; and that other beautiful 15th century bridge at Holme Bridge, two and a half miles further downstream. The parapets of both these bridges were damaged by armoured vehicles during the 1939–45 war, but have since been satisfactorily restored.

On the tidal reaches of the Frome lies the ancient township of Wareham, with its Georgian red brick houses and ancient church of St. Mary's. Wareham is a notable Dorset town of great antiquity. Five Christian inscriptions in the above church are in Latin, and are ascribed by experts to the seventh and eighth centuries; these seem to indicate the presence of a British (or what we would now term 'Welsh') Christian community at Wareham, which survived amid the Saxon influx in the late fifth and the sixth centuries. They indicate

The fine 15th century Holme bridge. The parapet has been renewed

also the certainty that Wareham dates back at least to Romano-British times. No doubt it was a port of significance at the head of Poole Harbour, and on an isthmus between the tidal reaches of Frome and Piddle. It remained so until mediaeval times, when the tidal channel of the estuary became partly silted up, and this, combined with an increase in the size and draught of ships, ended its function in this capacity. Poole had by then taken over as the main port of the district.

About the year 787, while, according to the Saxon Chronicle, 'the innocent English people, spread through their plains, were enjoying themselves in tranquillity and yoking their oxen to the plough', news was brought to the Reeve (Chief Magistrate) of Dorchester that a ship-load of strangers had landed close to Wareham. When he immediately rode to investigate this arrival, the strangers at once murdered him. This was the first recorded instance of the start of the Danish invasions, which were to be the scourge of England for the next two hundred and fifty years, finally providing a benificent Danish King of all England in the person of Canute, who embracing Christianity reigned from 1016 to 1035.

Under the Norman occupation, from 1066 onwards, Wareham continued to play its part as a small port. During the civil wars, at the time of Stephen and Matilda, great suffering was inflicted upon its inhabitants, it being recorded that the town changed hands no less than five times and was partly destroyed by sack, pillage and fire. Later it was recorded that it fulfilled its duty as a port by providing ships for King Edward III's Crecy expedition (1346) in the Hundred Years War, together with Poole and Lyme. These three ports produced altogether twenty-six ships manned by 479 men for this expedition.

At the time of the Civil War of the 17th century Wareham, like Poole and Dorchester, was strongly Parliamentarian in sympathy, but unlike Dorchester it was spared a sack by Royalist troops.

Later in the same century there was support in Wareham and its neighbourhood for the Duke of Monmouth's abortive effort to oust his uncle, King James II, from the throne. After the Battle of Sedgemoor (1685) and his Bloody Assizes in Dorchester, Judge Jefferies contrived in retaliation that some of Monmouth's supporters were hanged on Wareham's wall.

There are some fine buildings in Wareham, mostly of Georgian red brick, the prevalence of which is due to the rebuilding after the great fire of 1762, which destroyed much of this town to the extent of at least 113 houses.

Other reminders of past history in Wareham are the Black Bear Hotel, the designation of which indicates the popularity of bear baiting as a sport up to the eighteenth century, also the notice on the bridge over the Piddle, similar to those on the bridges at Sturminster Newton, Durweston, and Witchampton, threatening transportation as a penalty for wilful damage. These notices date back to the troubled era in Dorset as elsewhere of the 1820s and 1830s, but it is not recorded that the penalty was ever put into effect for this offence.

Perhaps the deterrent was sufficient!

Since that time Wareham has continued a peaceful career as a quiet Dorset country town, untroubled by outside disturbances, its present population numbering around 5,000. It remains to be seen whether the recent discovery of oil in its neighbourhood will bring about any unwelcome change in this enviable state of affairs.

Below Wareham the Frome has about a mile and a half of tidal estuary before it empties into the wide expanse of Poole Harbour, though in fact high tides affect the level of the river for nearly a mile upstream of Wareham. Poole Harbour is a tremendous natural inland expanse of salt water, about sixty miles round. It has a narrow outlet into the English Channel at Sandbanks, two miles from Poole itself. Poole was a thriving port in mediaeval times, until eventually most ships grew too large to enter its comparatively shallow waters.

Even so, during the nineteenth century sailing ships still harboured in it, many of them engaged in the Newfoundland trade. And right up to modern times it is still used by small coastal or cross-Channel vessels, and its Harbour provides moorings for a large number of minor pleasure craft.

The only fish caught in Poole Harbour nowadays, apart from a small number of salmon, grilse, and sea-trout are mullet, which appear there in numbers. During the seventeenth century, however, it was recorded that Brownsea Island, near the entrance to the Harbour, was a noted place for lobsters, crabs, and shrimps . . . unfortunately no longer. In the next century, too, Defoe recorded his admiration of Poole's oyster beds, now also a thing of the past.

FROME FISHING

Salmon

No doubt net fishing for salmon in the Frome dates back a long way. The first detailed records in Grimble's *The Salmon Rivers of England and Wales* (1904) go back to 1868, but Grimble refers also to net fishing long before that date. He also refers to a record in the old chronicles of Dorset that a century earlier salmon were so numerous that the officials of Wareham made a law that the apprentices of that town were not to be fed more than three times a week on these fish.

Stories of this sort, or on similar lines, are so common in so many different areas of Britain, where salmon rivers run through populated areas, that it might be assumed that there is some justifiable foundation for them. And if kelts were included as edible fish, (it was not made illegal to kill them until the 1860's), this would make objections to a surfeit of salmon all the more probable.

The old story has always persisted. Tradition has it that the clause was connected, in addition to Wareham, with such towns as London, Preston, Warrington, Kendal, Newcastle, Gloucester, Worcester, and Romsey amongst others. In the face of such widespread circumstantial evidence, it is hard to reject the story as baseless. Nevertheless, in spite of careful research, coupled with the offer of financial reward for its discovery, no such indenture or clause has ever in fact come to light, although the story sounds likely enough.

A quotation from *The Gentleman's Magazine* of as long ago as 1829 may be of interest in this connection:

'It is rather a pleasant task than otherwise to dispel illusions long current. An idea is prevalent that salmon were once so common in our great rivers that clauses were inserted in the indentures of apprentices to the effect that they should not be served as food more than twice, or thrice, a week.

Few statements have attained a wider ciruculation than this. I have myself heard the assertion made that such clauses existed not once but scores of times. Men with every claim to be regarded as authorities have advanced the statement again and again.

In innumerable books, the existence of this clause in an indenture is mentioned as being a thing well known and generally conceded. The theory indeed is extended to other countries. In Scotland it was said to be compulsory for a farmer to bind himself not to give his labourers salmon more than twice a week.

The most curious thing concerning the whole matter is that no proof of the existence of such an indenture can be found. Scores of people assert that they have seen it, and many have been sanguine as to their ability to lay their hands upon it. In no case whatever has it been forthcoming.'

And, as far as the author knows, no proof has been forthcoming since 1829; so readers are at liberty to believe what they like about this, both as regards Wareham apprentices and those elsewhere.

To return to Victorian times, by 1866 Grimble says that Frome salmon had been virtually wiped out by a bar net drawn across the river at Wareham and by fixed engines at East Stoke and Bindon Abbey. But the first Board of Conservators was formed in 1867, and thereafter things began gradually to improve.

A record of salmon and grilse catches in these early days of Frome fishing runs as follows:

'1868 to 1877—An average of 32 fish netted each season. Their average weight was 12 lb.
The first rod-caught salmon weighed 25 lb and was caught in 1877.'

It is interesting to note the comparatively small average size of the netted fish of this decade. Possibly this may have been because little netting was done until the summer, so that the big spring fish escaped. It is impossible now to say; and in any case, the curtain then falls until 1892, because reliable records are not available for the intervening period.

From 1892 onwards the record of Frome salmon and grilse catches continues as follows :

Date	Nets (yearly average)	Rods (yearly average)
1892–1901	36	6
1902–1911	13	8
1912–1921	104	104
1922–1931	58	172
1932–1941	74	254
1942–1951	82	168
1952–1961	95	357
1962–1971	148	335
1972–1976	108	254
1977–1981	66	269
1982	8	187
1983	23	230
1984	73	258
1985	86	236

The Frome rod fishing season lasts from March 1st until September 30th, starting a month later than that of the Avon.

The two highest rod catches were in 1963 when 692 salmon and grilse were killed, and in 1955 with 499. It will be noted that catches have declined over the past twenty-five years, but not markedly so. On the other hand, it must be remembered that since the 1930's rods have at least trebled in number, and fishing has become much more intensive here, as on other rivers.

Also it should be noted that the net catch in Poole Harbour would include a certain number of Piddle fish, impossible to identify. Compared to Frome fish, however, these are unlikely to have been numerous.

What definitely has occurred on the Frome, in counterpart to the Avon, is that during the past twenty-five or so years fish have become much smaller in average size. Spring salmon in the Frome during the first half of the 20th century used to average around 20 lb, just as they did on the Avon. Thirty pounders were common, and forty pounders not too rare. Before the 1939 war, fishing was considered to be over by mid-June. Thereafter the weed grew too thick and the fish became stale. The big spring fish then formed the bulk of the catch. But since the 1950's a change similar to that in the Avon has taken place, as all experienced Frome fishermen know. By degrees the three and four sea-winter fish have become scarcer and scarcer. They are not yet extinct, but sad to say are greatly reduced in numbers. The main catch is now of smaller two sea-winter salmon and of grilse, and the average weight has fallen to around 11 lb. Spring fishing is largely unproductive, but summer fishing has greatly improved, lasting even into August given reasonable weather.

Another change, which has lately become more apparent, is that many of the later running fish seem nowadays to stay downstream of Holme Bridge and in the lower part of the river near Wareham until the approach of the spawning season in October or November. They then move upstream in numbers, and the main spawning grounds are between Wool and Dorchester and up the Tadnol Brook. (Only odd redds are to be found below Wool or in the headwaters.) There is no apparent reason why fish should hesitate in this way to run upstream. There are no hatches or other obstructions in their path. Nevertheless, year after year they now tend to do so to the disadvantage of the fishing on the upper beats above Holme Bridge. There would seem to be no remedy for this, except patience and a hope of increased fish stocks in the future. At the same time, this situation obviously may well be advantageous to the fishing in the lower reaches.

Netting in the Frome during this present century has never abstracted an unduly large proportion of the stock. In fact, its return of catches has normally been smaller than that of the rods (see page 193). The present ownership of the main netting rights in the Frome lies in the hands of the Wessex Water Authority, which in the interests of fish conservation does not now exercise these rights at all. One independent net works in Poole Harbour, otherwise the Frome is not netted. Few rivers are so fortunate.

Apart from the natural river hazards common to salmon in their juvenile life from the ova to the smolt stage, and from the wide variety of predators that they subsequently meet in the sea, coupled with high seas or coastal fishing off Greenland, the Faroes, and Ireland, Frome salmon face perhaps less than the normal run of dangers. In the river itself pike are probably their worst enemy during their young life. Brown trout and eels must also prey on fry and parr to some extent; and cormorants, herons, and gulls no doubt take their toll. Sporadic net poaching is not unknown in Poole Harbour as well as in the neighbourhood of the estuary and off the nearby coast, but its effects are not extensive. There are no obstacles in the river which check the upstream passage of adult salmon or their downstream passage as smolts. The only other danger in any way likely is the possible ill effect of pollution at Dorchester or elsewhere, but this too is minimal and well under control. By and large, salmon in the Frome are therefore fortunate in their environment, and it is perhaps surprising that the annual rod catch is not higher.

In days gone by, as already noted, Frome salmon often ran large. There are endless records available to show this. One of them, for instance, is from W. Earl Hodgson's *Salmon Fishing* (1927), where the author writes: 'The average weight of salmon killed on the Frome has always been remarkably good, The five fish caught by myself in 1905 were no exception to this rule. The average weight was just under thirty pounds. The largest, a fine salmon, weighed 41 lb, the smallest 22 lb. All were taken on fly.' What British river nowadays could produce anything approaching such an average weight?

The record rod-caught Frome fish weighed 49 lb and was taken in the 1930's; but many other 40 pounders were accounted for at this time. Mr. R. C. Hardy-Corfe, a noted Frome fisherman of that period, had a fishing cottage at Holme Bridge, and his sitting room there held models of seven 40 pounders, which he himself had taken on the Frome. The biggest was of $48\frac{1}{2}$ lb. These fish had all been caught on bait of one sort or another, except for one of 41 lb on fly. R. H. C. used to describe this one as 'a very big fish for a fly', which so far as the Frome was concerned was certainly true. 'Corfie', as he was known to his friends was a most kindly patient and considerate person, always ready to help over anything to do with fishing as with anything else. He was an outstanding Frome fisherman of

This photograph, taken in 1938, shows Robert Hardy-Corfe, a giant amongst the Frome fishermen of his day, fishing the Lower Horseshoe pool on the Frome at East Stoke. He is prawning, with an uptrace spinner and wire trace. His rod is a powerful split cane bait-rod of 9 foot 6 inches in length, and his reel (not visible in this photo) a Silex Major. This was his usual bait-fishing outfit, and he was a deadly performer with it. The gaff on his back was telescopic and would extend to about nine feet in length, a useful implement for gaffing a fish when he was single-handed. When this photo was taken, he had just located a fish. His absorbtion is obvious, and he would have been prepared to spend a long time tantalizing it if necessary. He did in fact hook this fish and eventually landed it, weight 15 lb.

his day, though he sometimes fished at Delfur on the Spey, and on the Dee also. A good fly fisher, he was better still with a bait, and particularly with a prawn fished with an 'uptrace' spinner. When he had a fish marked down he would spend hours tantalizing it, and would almost always persuade it to take in the end. He fished mainly at East Stoke, but knew all the river at least from Bindon downstream like the back of his hand. There is still a pool named after him on the Bindon water. As a matter of interest, 'Corfie' also shared with a friend, Mr. M. R. L. White, a magnificent single day's catch of rudd from the Ravensthorpe reservoir in the midlands. The bag consisted of 140 fish weighing 170 lb, many of them between 2 and $2\frac{1}{2}$ lb. All these fish were caught on fly, mainly a dry fly. As well as his salmon models, Corfie had on his sitting room wall a glass case containing two or three stuffed specimens of these rudd.

Salmon fishing on the Frome extends basically over the bottom fourteen miles of river, from Moreton to just above Wareham. Above Moreton only odd fish are caught. In character the Frome is much like the lower Avon, and runs at about the same speed. But it is only half the size of the Avon, i.e. half its width (although nearly as deep in some places). It is therefore very easy for the angler, unless his casting is accurate, to hook the opposite bank, particularly when he is trying to pitch his fly or bait very close to it, as is often necessary. In summer, trees and undergrowth along the Frome's banks sometimes grow up thickly and form a constant series of traps for the careless caster. The average width of this river is only about ten yards, so it can be realized how important is ability on the part of the angler to cast with great precision.

Weed growth in the Frome is similar to that of most other south-country rivers. In summer the growth is thick and fast, and if not cut it causes flooding in the adjacent water meadows. There are organized weed cutting periods as on the Avon, and this system works reasonably well. On the lower part of the river, the Water Authority cuts the weeds by boat and removes the cut weed from the river; while on the upper river riparian owners cut their own weed. Curiously enough, salmon like the growing weed. It gives them shade and shelter, and they prefer a stretch of water with good weed growth to one that for one reason or another is bare of it. Weed clumps also constrict the flow into narrow channels in places, where the increased current ensures a clear gravel bottom and thus a probable lie for fish. Also growing weed helps in daylight to oxygenate the water. It does therefore provide a number of advantages.

Like other chalk rivers, the Frome varies little in height, and does not rise or fall quickly. So far as fishing is concerned, the height of water therefore makes no great difference, and even at low summer level there are still plenty of lies in fair fishing order, provided they do not become choked with weed. The water is naturally fairly clear, though after heavy rain the run-off from the sandy tank-training ground at Bovington is apt to discolour the whole river from Wool downstream; a tiresome though inevitable drawback, as it puts an end to fishing for the time being if too excessive.

Luxuriant water meadows lie alongside all the lower Frome, as they do further upstream, a haven for wildlife and birds of many sorts. On the southern skyline is the soft swell of the Purbeck Hills. The whole setting is one of peace and tranquility—highly welcome in these present days of haste and turmoil. There are hatches at East Stoke and Bindon, but these present no obstacle to fish, being kept wide open. Incidentally, it is a curious fact that hatch pools such as the one at Bindon, although they look like certain holding places either in their main stream or back wash, very seldom produce fish. For some reason salmon do not lie there; perhaps the current is too strong or too turbulent, or there is something wrong with the forma-tion of the river-bed. Whatever the cause may be, only one or two salmon at the most are caught in Bindon hatch pool each season. There are also hatches at Moreton and others above, but they too do not hold up the fish to any extent.

While a few redds are to be found higher up or lower down, the main salmon spawning area in the Frome lies in the middle reaches between Wool Bridge and Dorchester, also up the Tadnol Brook. The young fry and parr in this area have to compete with an extensive brown trout stock, also they are preyed upon by pike; but this again is inevitable. It is perhaps curious that more salmon do not spawn further upstream in the headwaters (though doubtless they would be unwelcome to trout fishermen). They appear to prefer the middle reaches.

As to the smolt migration to the sea, recent investigations have shown that the large majority of smolts in the Frome, as in the Avon

A 23 lb April fish at Bindon

(see page 65), are of one year in age. This quick development no doubt results from the exceptionally luscious feed which fry and parr obtain in chalk rivers.

The problem of pollution hardly arises in the Frome. Dorchester and Wareham are the only sizeable towns on its course, and their sewage is efficiently treated. Twenty or so years ago there was an unfortunate case of pollution which was said to have killed all fish in the river from Wool down to Wareham; but any ill effects of this have by now worn off. Otherwise, the Frome has always been remarkably pure, apart from the occasional minor lapses due to farm sewage or toxic spray.

Nor has the Frome been afflicted by that scourge of the past twenty years, the disease U.D.N. None of the south-country rivers have, east of the Exe. Devonshire rivers on the other hand have suffered catastrophically. It seems likely that this is due to their acidity, rising as they do in the peat soil of Dartmoor or Exmoor; whereas the chalk salmon rivers, Frome, Avon, Test and Itchen are all pronouncedly alkaline. They are U.D.N.-free, and always have been, presumably for this reason.

The process of rod fishing for salmon in the Frome is very much the same with the same tackle as in the Avon (see page 69). Bait fishing is the more effective method rather than fly-fishing, and for the same reasons as in the Avon. Fishing the prawn is particularly successful, especially in the deep holes in summer, when the weed has grown up all round. It can be fished 'sink and draw', or else spun. A Devon

Aylmer Tryon playing a fish, river Frome

minnow earlier in the year is a good bait, or a Toby spoon. When the stream lessens in summer, a Mepps spoon spins and shows up well. It is always advisable for the angler to carry a gaff. The banks are almost always high and steep, which makes landing fish difficult, and there is always the chance of an outsized fish, too big for a single handed landing net. There is no need for wading. Gumboots or their equivalent are all that are needed for footwear, all fishing being from the bank or, at the most, from ankle deep stance in the water off a sand bank or mud flat. The necessity for accurate casting has already been mentioned; and there is particular need in such a small river for the angler to keep out of sight of the fish. He should take special pains to do so. It is too late when he sees the fine bow wave of a frightened fish heading up or down river and probably scaring others of his kind. A sizeable salmon makes a considerable disturbance in its flight, when it swims away fast in a small river such as this one.

Catherine Wills fly fishing for salmon at Bindon

Fly fishing in the Frome is by no means impossible, though eleven out of every twelve Frome fish are probably now caught on bait, mainly because it is much more often used. As soon as the water is reasonably warm Frome salmon will take a fly quite well, though its use is subject to the same limitations as in the Avon (see page 72). The narrowness of this river is an even greater handicap to the effective use of the fly than in the wider Avon. Yet Aylmer Tryon once caught five fish on a fly before breakfast one day in the 1960's at Bindon, and a sixth fish later in the same morning. So it can be done! though it is doubtful whether any other Frome fly fisherman has ever achieved such outstanding success. Nowadays one is doing well to catch even a single fish in a day on a fly, two is excellent, and three or four beyond all likelihood.

As to tackle, in the spring with high or fairly high water a rod of not less than fourteen feet is advisable, with a large fly fished well sunk. Later on, with the approach of summer, and with a floating line and smaller fly, the rod length can be reduced; and for those who like single-handed rods, a carbon rod of as little as ten feet may be found adequate, though many fishermen might prefer a double-handed one of twelve or thirteen feet. It would be a matter of personal inclination. As in the Avon, the size of fly need never be unduly small. Size 6 is quite small enough at any time, and a larger one may well be preferable as the water in the lower part of the river is seldom now completely clear, there being usually some degree of cloudiness. Pattern of fly matters little, though a hair wing is probably best, or something in the nature of a shrimp fly, scantily dressed.

The main salmon fisheries on the Frome at the time of writing are as follows. At the top is Moreton, some four miles upstream of Wool. This fishing consists of two beats, with a maximum of two rods per beat. It has fishing on both banks for a distance of about two miles.

Next below comes East Burton, with three miles of fishing, divided into four beats for one rod apiece. This fishery too has both banks throughout its length.

Below this is the Wool Bridge Manor water leased from Cdr. Walter Drax, on the left bank only, for about one and a half miles. The opposite bank belongs to the Weld Estate.

The Bindon Abbey water, also belonging to the Weld Estate, follows. This beat for the past thirty years has been let to the Hon. Aylmer Tryon. It has fishing on the right bank alone for most of its two miles length, but a short distance on the left bank also on its upper section. The opposite bank is separately owned by Mrs. Fuller and Mrs. Rees Reynolds.

Downstream of Bindon, the Freshwater Biological Society owns the East Stoke water, which extends for about two and a half miles on both banks. Up to seven rods at a time fish here.

This brings one to Holme Bridge, at which lies the Longmead fishing for two rods on the left bank, with the Joint Water also for two rods on the right. Below this the Priory water for four rods extends to close to the disused Swanage railway bridge, while a stretch of about a mile on the left bank above Wareham belongs to Cdr. Walter Drax. Downstream of this the Frome is increasingly affected by the tide, and little fishing is done.

Sea-trout on the Frome

Like all south-country rivers, the Frome has a run of sea-trout, though they are not apparently very numerous, or perhaps not greatly sought after. The record of sea-trout rod catches in recent years runs as follows:

1970 – 49	1978 – 195
1971 – 39	1979 – 89
1972 – 27	1980 – 253
1973 – 123	1981 – 111
1974 – 139	1982 – 91
1975 – 208	1983 – 87
1976 – 48	1984 – 96
1977 – 63	1985 – 70

N.B. Most of these sea-trout are normally taken low down in the river near Wareham, or at least below Holme Bridge. The sea-trout rod fishing season lasts from April 15th to October 31st each year. The average weight of these fish varies little, it is around 2 lb.

Bigger fish of up to 10 lb or over are sometimes caught. Notable examples include a fish of $22\frac{1}{2}$ lb taken above the hatches at Bindon by S. R. Dwight in May, 1946; also one of 21 lb by R. C. Hardy-Corfe in 1918. Aylmer Tryon caught one of $15\frac{1}{2}$ lb and Mr. C. R. Rothwell one of 15 lb at Bindon in May, 1981 both on fly. There have been others of large size, but unfortunately all these latter fish were taken on strong salmon tackle, when their captors were salmon fishing; so the kudos attached to their capture was thereby lessened. On the other hand, the present Lord Tryon in July 1954 caught a beautiful sea-trout of 8 lb in the hatch pool at Bindon, and this one was on a small sedge fished on light dry fly tackle. It took half an hour to land, and was his first sea-trout.

Sea-trout in Poole Harbour are also caught by net, but the returns on this form of fishing show a catch of less than that of the Frome rods. (It is possible, however, that these returns in the past have not been completely accurate, and they would also include some Piddle fish.)

The return of sea-trout, net caught over recent years, runs as follows:

1970 – 66	1978 – 137
1971 – 56	1979 – 50
1972 – 45	1980 – 73
1973 – 85	1981 – 72
1974 – 10	1982 – 51
1975 – 138	1983 – 31
1976 – 77	1984 – 58
1977 – 118	1985 – 54

The average weight of these net caught fish is around 4 lb, higher than the average weight of rod caught fish because most of the smaller sized fish escape through the net meshes, which are large enough in size to allow this. Also net fishing ceases at the end of July; while in August and thereafter sea-trout of smaller size continue to run, and some are caught by rod, thus reducing the overall average rod-caught weight.

As a whole, therefore, the Frome can in no way be classed as a great sea-trout river (in spite of having produced a $22\frac{1}{2}$ pounder, the record rod-caught sea-trout for the British Isles, also a 21 pounder.) Nor indeed does it have the appearance of one. Nevertheless, big sea-trout, and the biggest fish usually run early, can sometimes be seen rising to the mayfly, in late May or early June, a sight to gladden any dry fly fisherman's heart. (So for that matter can salmon, which is even more exciting.)

Coarse Fish on the Frome

There is no recognized coarse fishing in this river, as there is in the Avon and Stour. In addition, almost all coarse fish downstream of Wool (except those in side streams) were killed by the pollution twenty years ago, mentioned above.

To some extent they have recovered by now, and grayling and pike are to be found in this part of the river, together with occasional fish of other sorts. Eels, of course, proliferate, as they do in all these rivers. Pike are a menace both to young salmon and brown trout. If not kept down, they would undoubtedly increase rapidly. They tend to be more numerous in the middle reaches of the river between Dorchester and Wool, but their numbers are kept in check by periodic electric fishing. A big pike of 27 lb caught recently by this method had a grilse of 5 lb inside it.

In days gone by it seems that the Frome harboured a large number of coarse fish including pike, some of them big ones. For instance Major Radclyffe of Hyde House says (in 1903): 'The river is literally swarming with coarse fish amongst which are heavy pike, with a good few otters on the banks. . . . Scarcely any fry hatched in the river live to get to the sea.' Also an outstanding day's pike fishing on the Frome was described by Alfred Jardine, the great coarse fisherman of that period, in 'The Sportsman' of 1894. The weather was exceptionally cold that day, and the fish took the live bait well, though the lines were apt to get clogged with beads of ice. The writer described the sport as 'simply magnificent', with many big fish killed in spite of the bitter weather, though he did not mention actual numbers. In those days it was unlikely that any effort was made by owners of fishings to keep the pike down. The only means of doing so at that time, apart from rod-fishing or snaring, would have been by netting, a method which even if it was practised would have been far from thorough. The result would have been a plentiful stock of pike in the river, as Jardine implies, to the detriment of other fish.

Mullet in Poole Harbour have already been mentioned. These fish in summer run up the Frome, certainly as far as the hatch pool at Bindon, where they can sometimes be seen lying in shoals. They seem to average from two to three pounds in weight. For angling purposes they are worthless, as they apparently feed, if at all in fresh-water, only on weed. But they are said to be quite good from a culinary point of view. They appear to prefer lying in still water or backwaters, and so far as is known are harmless to other fish.

An unusual fish caught by rod in the Frome in the early 1900's was a sturgeon, weighing 203 lb. This fish was stuffed and used to be on exhibit in the Dorchester Museum, but unfortunately it has now been removed.

The following account of the capture of this fish is given by Major Eustace Radclyffe in his book 'Round the Smoking Room Fire':

'I managed to foul-hook it with a big salmon fly and after a terrific fight killed it. It was 9 ft 5 ins long and weighed 203 lb. It is I believe the largest fish ever killed in a British river. I presented the fish to King Edward VII, but it was afterwards stuffed.'

Mrs. Audrey Radclyffe, herself an excellent fisher as well as a champion dog-handler, and to whom the author of this present book is indebted for the information about this remarkable event, adds: 'Eustace was my brother-in-law, and lived at Hyde House not far from Wareham but on the Piddle. I saw the sturgeon in his museum there, but Hyde House was later sold. I do not know the exact date it was caught, but this was at Bindon, and I believe it was in a putrid state when it reached the King, who sent it back!'

It was indeed amazing that this huge fish should have penetrated some nine miles up a comparatively small river, passing through the hatches at East Stoke en route. As to Major Radclyffe's battle with it, this can only be left to the imagination! 'Round the Smoking Room Fire' is long out of print; but it makes good reading for anyone interested in field sports who can obtain a copy. One of the amusing anecdotes concerns Major Radclyffe's retriever, which he had trained to take the place of a landing net in retrieving hooked trout, when played out, from the water.

Major Radclyffe's dog retrieving a fish for him!

Trout Fishing on the Frome

Last, but not least, a word or two about Frome brown trout fishing, since it is as a dry-fly river for brown trout that this river is perhaps best renowned. There are plenty of brown trout in its headwaters and a number of privately owned fisheries there, but the best of its fishing starts in the neighbourhood of Gascoyne Bridge about two miles upstream of Dorchester, below the entry of the Sydling brook near Frampton, and subsequently with the main stream reinforced by the Cerne near Charminster. It would be hard to imagine a more perfect chalk stream, in a more delightful and unspoilt setting. First class trout fishing extends downstream to Hurst Bridge, immediately above Moreton, over a distance of about 13 miles of river. It is good water all the way, whether in main stream or side streams, and produces an excellent catch of sizeable trout, with two to three pounders not uncommon, and occasionally even larger fish (see p. 212). Even the little Sydling Brook and Cerne Brook produce good trout in their lower reaches.

Above Gascoyne Bridge the best fishing belongs to Mr. C. Pope of Wrackleford House, who owns a fine stretch of water there. Then from Gascoyne Bridge down to Dorchester, and again for some two miles further downstream almost as far as Lower Bockhampton, the Dorchester Fishing Club own or lease the fishing, which covers some five miles of water altogether, the bottom stretch of right bank being rented from Brigadier S. N. Floyer Acland. Below this lies the West Stafford Estate water, belonging also to Brigadier S. N. Floyer Acland, and divided into two sections by Mr. R. Belgrove's and Mr. R. Pavitt's water. Downstream of West Stafford lies the Herringstone Estate water belonging to Major General A. Williams, and Mr. J. Eyles' Lewell Mill Water.

The Ilsington Estate fishings then follow, extending as far as Nine Hatches, and below these are the Woodsford Manor fishings belonging to Mr. W. Paul. Below this Mr. Paul and Mr. Lovett have opposite

Upper Frome above Dorchester

banks as far as Pallington, while in the Pallington Farm area Brigadier C. M. F. Webb and Mr. H. Mekin have opposite banks. Below Pallington Farm, and as far as Hurst Bridge, Mr. Paul continues on the south bank and Mr. Mekin on the north. This brings one to the Moreton fishing which is more closely concerned with salmon, and it really marks the end of the good trout water. Below this, the river becomes wider and deeper, and although big trout may occasionally be caught on the mayfly, they are scarce. Spawning conditions no doubt deteriorate, and as mentioned above all resident fish below Wool were killed some years ago through a bad case of pollution. These included any brown trout in that part of the river—and they have never recovered. Experiments have been made with artificial stocking in the lower river on a number of occasions, but in every case the stocked trout have virtually disappeared after a short interval. One is forced to the conclusion that brown trout in the lower part of the Frome do not maintain themselves successfully.

A view of the Upper Frome

Above Moreton, however, things become different, and both wild trout and stocked trout are plentiful. One must conclude, so far as wild trout are concerned, that provided vermin are kept down, pollution prevented, and fishing properly regulated, it is the presence of suitable and widespread spawning grounds which makes the whole difference to stocks. The upper Frome bears eloquent testimony to this principle.

There is a good fly hatch on the upper half of the river, an unlimited benefit so far as dry-fly fishing is concerned, with plentiful mayfly during the last two weeks of May and early June. Even as late a period of the season as September can often produce substantial hatches of small fly.

Weed growth is abundant, with plentiful ranunculus as well as other sorts of good weed. On the other hand, in the water below

Dorchester, there has recently been an excessive growth of the weed known as water dropwort or water parsley. This has lately proliferated to a totally unwelcome extent, its white flower heads rising high above the water surface. It is inclined to grow so thickly as to block the entire channel of the river. The cause of such profuse growth is unknown, and the only satisfactory remedy is the laborious one of extraction by hand, a back-breaking and lengthy process, though very necessary.

Weed cutting on the upper river is left to riparian owners. Lower down, as mentioned above, the Water Authority both cut the weed with their specially equipped boat, and extract the cut weed, using a drag-line.

Water abstraction is not at the moment a pressing problem on the Frome. In 1971 a month long enquiry at Dorchester resulted in the refusal of a proposal to abstract up to six million gallons daily from a bore-hole in the Sydling valley. A potential menace to the flow of the Frome was thus, fortunately, averted.

Coarse fish too are no great problem in the Frome trout waters, with the one exception of pike. Though as in all chalk rivers these predators seldom permeate right to the headwaters, in the reaches below Dorchester they everywhere proliferate if given the chance (see p. 205). Pike are a permanent menace to brown trout and exert a perpetual toll on them. The two best ways of keeping their numbers down are undoubtedly by electric D.C. fishing, efficiently conducted, and by the use of wire cage traps. The old fashioned process of netting seldom produces good results.

Salmon arrive upstream of Moreton, but principally in spawning time after the fishing season is over. Only occasional fish are caught in this part of the river earlier on. The main salmon spawning area in the Frome as mentioned above does however lie between Wool and Dorchester, and up the Tadnol Brook.

Mention should be made of one quite exceptional brown trout hooked and landed in the past a short distance below Dorchester. This was the Rev. S. E. V. Filleul's fish of 12¾ lb, caught in 1907 on a small dry fly. A washing basket had to be used to help in landing this outsized trout, as an ordinary landing net was quite inadequate. It is thought to be the biggest brown trout ever caught in Britain on an orthodox dry fly. (Bigger brown trout certainly have been caught, but always on bait or some lure other than a proper dry fly.) This was a remarkable feat, considering also that the fish in question was a wild one, and not a stew bred fish reared to a large size before being introduced into a river or lake on the modern pattern. It was stuffed, and is now in the possession of Mr. H. Wood-Homer of Bardolf Manor, near Puddletown, the Rev. Filleul's grandson. It is a short but remarkably thick fish of exceptional girth. What are just as remarkable are the gut cast tapered to size 4x and the dry fly, a Greenwell's Glory, size 10, on which this trout was landed. They were mounted in the glass case with their victim. It apparently took the best part of an hour to land this fish, an almost incredible achievement on such fine tackle.

CONCLUSION

This brings to an end my reflections on these beloved Wessex rivers and their surroundings. A sense of history long past broods over them; such names as Sarum, Ringwood, Christchurch, Blandford Forum, Wimborne Minster, Dorchester and Wareham carry us back from modern times towards the dawn of civilization in this island. Even before the arrival of the Romans, an organized life was being carried on in these river valleys, and ever since those long-ago days such rivers and their tributaries have remained as arteries in the flow of life in the Wessex countryside.

Anyone born and bred in this area can hardly fail to find of absorbing interest the varied aspects of local river life, whether this relates to beast, fish, or fowl, or whether to trees, or weeds or flowers on the bank or in the water. Who, for instance, when walking across a bridge can forbear to stop and examine the river's flow both upstream and downstream? and who can resist pausing at a hatch pool to contemplate the downward rush of white water, the mysterious depths of the midstream, and the quickening glide of the outlet? As James Hogg sang in praise of the fascination of wild water's flow:

'Where the pools are bright and deep,
Where the grey trout lies asleep,
Up the river and over the lea,
That's the way for Billie and me.'

This, and the remainder of his 'Boy's Song', resolves it all so admirably.

Urbanization is the greatest danger in modern times to the natural character of our rivers and to their purity. Urbanization is apt to lead to pollution, water abstraction, semi-canalization through large-scale dredging, industrialization with housebuilding close to the riverside, and other attendant afflictions. The peace and beauty which are the birthright of our river systems can so easily be

213

destroyed in this modern age. Even in the remote countryside there also exist dangers, the rapid growth of large fish farms for instance, or pollution from farm sewage or toxic spray, as well as bore-holes which in response to the ever increasing demand denude river beds of water. Indeed there are many problems to be solved and many difficulties facing such responsible bodies as the Water Authorities, as well as individual riparian owners, if the attractions of our native rivers are to be preserved for the benefit of ourselves and our descendants. As fast as one problem is settled, as is only to be expected in this modern fast changing world, another seems at once to arise. The struggle is never ending.

If my readers have persevered to the end of this book, or even part-way through it, I am grateful to them, and hope they have found something to their interest. I hope too that they have found no errors in the text; but if they have, and if they do not always agree with all I have said, I ask their forbearance.

J. A. C.

Index

220   INDEX